To Barbara —

Thank you for saying hello!

— [signature]

2.1.11

Praise for *Prove It Before You Promote It*

"*Prove It Before You Promote It* shows how to spot and avoid thinking traps, take a critical look at the evidence, and apply scientific criteria to the charting of an intelligent course. The more marketers—or, for that matter, people in general—learn to do that, the better off we'll all be. Your challenge awaits. Read this book if you dare . . . "

> —Dr. Michael Shermer, Executive Director, Skeptics Society; Contributing Editor and monthly columnist, *Scientific American*; bestselling author of *The Mind of the Market*, *The Science of Good and Evil*, and *Science Friction*

"*Prove It Before You Promote It* will inform you, entertain you, challenge your assumptions, even infuriate you. Read this book and I guarantee you will never approach research and marketing in quite the same way ever again."

> —Brian Rasmussen, Managing Director, R&R Partners, creators of the famous Las Vegas campaign, "What happens here stays here"

"At last—a practical way to know, once and for all, what your advertising dollar buys. It's about time someone wrote this book. Ignore it at your peril."

> —Adrian Gostick, author of the *New York Times* bestseller *The Carrot Principle*

"Steve Cuno challenges the conventions of the advertising agency business with every turn of the page. In fact, this book passes the same test as a great ad: you either like it or dislike it, but you certainly won't feel neutral about it."

—Tim Williams, President, Ignition Consulting Group

"A stunningly candid exposé on marketing decision-making. *Prove It Before You Promote It* re-enthrones the measurable objective, and rescues marketers from inadvertently derailing themselves due to reliance on a self-indulgent gut. Steve Cuno lays a solid foundation for the successful execution of a variety of campaigns, from acquisition to loyalty marketing.

No more focus groups of one! Steve has convinced me that a regime of objective setting, disciplined testing, and continual measurement are the keys to marketing success and profitability in the modern business."

—Bill Hanifin, Managing Director,
Customer Growth LLC

"Indispensable for my business clients who are contemplating spending scarce resources on a serious marketing effort."

—J. Steven Newton, Managing Attorney,
Business Law Associates, L.C.

Prove It Before You Promote It

Prove It Before You Promote It

How to Take the Guesswork Out of Marketing

Steve Cuno

WILEY

John Wiley & Sons, Inc.

Published by John Wiley & Sons, Inc., Hoboken, New Jersey.
Published simultaneously in Canada.

For general information on our other products and services or for technical support, please contact our Customer Care Department within the United States at (800) 762-2974, outside the United States at (317) 572-3993 or fax (317) 572-4002.

Wiley also publishes its books in a variety of electronic formats. Some content that appears in print may not be available in electronic books. For more information about Wiley products, visit our web site at www.wiley.com.

Library of Congress Cataloging-in-Publication Data:

Cuno, Steve, 1954–
    Prove it before you promote it : how to take the guesswork out of marketing/ Steve Cuno.
        p. cm.
    Includes bibliographical references and index.
    ISBN 978-0-470-38118-2 (cloth)
1. Marketing–Management.   2. Advertising–Management.
3. Marketing.   4. Advertising.   I. Title.
    HF5415.13.C855 2009
    658.8'3–dc22   2008020131

Printed in the United States of America.

10 9 8 7 6 5 4 3 2 1

To Paula Jane Tanner Cuno,
in loving memory

Also to Rebecca, Jeff, Scotty,
and the crew at RESPONSE

Contents

Foreword

That's Nice. Prove It!

MICHAEL SHERMER

The war in Iraq is now five years old. At a cost of $200 million a day, $73 billion a year, and over $350 billion since it began, plus over 4,000 American lives, that's a substantial investment. No wonder most members of Congress from both parties, along with President Bush, believe that we've got to "stay the course" and not just "cut and run." As Bush explained in a 4th of July, 2006, speech at Ft. Bragg, North Carolina: "I'm not going to allow the sacrifice of 2,527 troops who have died in Iraq to be in vain by pulling out before the job is done."

In the science of behavioral economics, this is what is known as the *sunk-cost fallacy*, by which we base decisions on how much cost we have sunk into something in the past rather than what it is actually worth doing or keeping to-day and tomorrow. In other words, we base our decisions on past investment rather than future value. We hang on to losing stocks, unprofitable investments, failing businesses, and unsuccessful relationships. If we were rational, we would just compute the odds of succeeding from this point forward and then decide whether the investment warrants the potential payoff. But we are not rational—not in love, or war, or business.

The sunk-cost fallacy is just one of numerous cognitive mistakes we make, proving once and for all that *Homo Economicus,* or *Economic Man,* is a myth. This myth holds that we are by nature rational, self-maximizing, and free; that is, when we make choices we rationally compute the odds for how to maximize our utility (or value), and we do so with complete free will. As I like to say when I encounter a claim of the paranormal or supernatural or miraculous or something else highly unusual in my job as the editor of *Skeptic* magazine, "That's nice. Prove it!"

In *Prove It Before You Promote It: How to Take the Guesswork Out of Marketing,* Steve Cuno has taken this new science of behavioral economics and applied it to the real world, demonstrating that before you can prove your marketing, you must countenance the possibility that the way you—and the industry at large—have always done things, the marketing tactics that "everyone knows" are effective, and the campaigns in which your company has heavily invested might not be producing the results you thought they were. One obstacle to this process of proving it before you promote it is another mental bias called "cognitive dissonance," discovered by the psychologist Leon Festinger when he investigated a UFO cult in the 1950s that believed that the world was going to come to an end and that they would be whisked away in the mother ship just in time. Festinger wanted to know what would happen when the world did not come to an end; that is, would the devoted followers admit they were wrong and pack up and go home. What he discovered was that the more invested the members were into the cult, the less likely they were to admit that they were wrong. In fact, most of the heavily invested group members became even more zealous in their recruitment of new members, insisting that the world really was coming to an end, but that they had just miscalculated the date.

Festinger called this phenomenon *cognitive dissonance*, and it applies to many walks of life, making it next to impossible for any of us to admit we are wrong. Who among us routinely says, "I was wrong" or "I made a mistake"? At best, most people will confess something closer to "mistakes were made." The passive past tense of the all-telling phrase—*mistakes were made*—shows the rationalization process at work. "Mistakes were quite possibly made by the administrations in which I served," confessed Henry Kissinger about Vietnam, Cambodia, and South America. "If, in hindsight, we also discover that mistakes may have been made . . . I am deeply sorry," admitted Cardinal Edward Egan of New York about the Catholic Church's failure to deal with pedophile priests.

No one is immune from cognitive dissonance, including, and especially, marketers. Like anyone else, the more time and money marketers invest in a campaign, the more fiercely they will defend it, regardless of results or, more often, of their obliviousness to them. No marketer would disagree that the people they target with their marketing make irrational purchasing decisions. Indeed, marketers count on it and load promotions with emotional appeals. People are for the most part unaware of what motivates their behavior. As I point out in my book, *The Mind of the Market: Compassionate Apes, Compulsive Humans, and Other Tales from Evolutionary Economics,* Economic Man does not exhibit unbounded rationality, self-interest, free will, or efficiency in decisions and choices. Indeed, motivators be-hind many of our decisions are the products of behaviors we evolved in an environment substantially different from the one we now inhabit. For instance, our predilection to eat more foods that taste sweet may not be rational today (given the obesity epidemic), but likely served us well as hunter-gatherers in need of the nutrients found in fruits.

Though marketers readily admit that their target market doesn't purchase rationally, the trick for marketers is to avoid irrational decision making themselves when it's *their* turn to be the customer as they weigh buying into a mar-keting program. For instance, there is a prevalent belief among marketers that the successful practice of their craft is rooted in a magical, intuitive sixth sense. They know what works because they're the experts. The tautology—an argument using itself as proof—goes largely unchallenged. Another oft-unchallenged belief revolves around *creativity*, a mystical black box deemed ultimately responsible for marketing successes and held blameless in the wake of marketing failures. Advertising agencies claim their cre-ativity beats any competitor's creativity, yet no one seems to be able to quantify it. Many agencies go so far as to argue that attempting to do so is a blasphemy that strips the cre-ative process of its power.

This book invites marketers to abandon these and other fallacies and then shows you how to replace them with facts. But that first step matters. If you're going to prove your marketing, you must be willing to disprove it. Mar-keters tend to view their field as an art, and as such it's not unusual for them to resist melding it with science. It goes both ways. Most scientists, especially social scientists, resist attempts to apply evolutionary thinking outside the strict bounds of biology. But to truly understand human behavior, we must study it in all areas, including economics and marketing, just as the physicist, chemist, or biologist studies the laws of nature. It is to bridging that gap that I have dedicated much of my own work as a scientist.

Steve Cuno has logged 30-plus years in the field of marketing. He is also a member of the Skeptics Society, of which I am the founder and executive director. The Skeptics Society is a scientific and educational organization devoted to the study of controversial ideas, extraordinary claims, and revolutionary ideas. Not to be confused with the cynic, who rejects everything as a matter of course, the skeptic takes a step back and examines the evidence before accepting or rejecting.

This combination makes Steve a skeptical marketer. I hope you'll agree with me that that's a good thing, even though heresies inevitably come with the skeptical territory. Steve dares to commit a number of them in *Prove It Before You Promote It*. He shows that like anyone, marketers are subject to logical fallacies that when unrecognized and unabated waste budgets. He debunks creativity as the god in the marketing gap. He pokes holes in marketing research. He takes on your favorite business writers. He presents convincing evidence that marketing can and should be brought into the realm of measurable science. But far from assailing and dismantling, the net result is clear direction for sound and scientifically based marketing.

Prove It Before You Promote It shows how to spot and avoid thinking traps, take a critical look at the evidence, and apply scientific criteria to the charting of an intelligent course. The more marketers—or, for that matter, people in general—learn to do that, the better off we'll all be.

Your challenge awaits. Read this book if you dare. . . .

—Michael Shermer

Preface

Something a bit oxymoronic seems to happen when sales plummet. Folks in top management start to talk about cutting the marketing budget.

"Wait!" we marketing and advertising people cry. "When sales are down, you should *increase* marketing!"[1] We characterize executives who turn a greedy eye on the marketing budget as myopic bean counters. Cutting marketing because sales are down, we plead, is like cutting insulin because the patient's diabetes has gotten worse.

But such pleas are based on the postulate that we end up with more beans with marketing than we would without it. And that poses a problem, because postulates are *assumptions,* not fact. Perhaps cutting the marketing budget when sales are down isn't myopia so much as a tacit rejection of the postulate.

Such a rejection wouldn't be wholly unjustified. Few companies track the effectiveness of their marketing, let alone their advertising, and most who try do a woeful job. A small number measure campaign awareness, but inferring an increase in beans from an increase in awareness only supports another unproved postulate. The vast majority of companies rely on far less formal, equally impotent defenses of the craft: they like their ads, the board likes the ads, and the neighbor who saw the ads said they were cool. Justifying marketing and advertising in those terms renders them more of an egocentric luxury than a business necessity. No wonder that when times get tough, marketing budgets get axed right along with the other fluff.

Perhaps, as a dedicated marketer, your first priority isn't saving your hide but rather contributing to the overall good of the company. Either way, you might want to note that it's a lot harder for the Powers That Be to cut a program that produces in reality than one that produces in theory.

So why don't more marketers prove the effectiveness of their work *in reality?* Ah, that's an interesting question. Many seem to think it can't be done. Early in my career when I worked on the client side, I asked my ad agency to explain why they were confident their ad campaign was going to sell my product, and how we'd measure how much it sold. The account executive said, "Ads don't sell per se, so you really can't measure them that way. Ads create an impression that people act on later without really knowing why." Now that's just nonsense, but it's also the typical ad agency spiel. Somehow, we are to trust that marketing and advertising work a kind of magic that is beyond—even above—accountability. It's an art, a certain *je ne sais quoi.* Like a medium holding a séance, many ad people caution you not to mess with the magic or you'll offend the spirits who then won't cooperate. Ask how many widgets the campaign sold, and expect someone to disdainfully explain to you that it's not that simple.

News flash: It really is that simple. Advertising can sell, per se and all. *That's what it was invented to do.* And advertising *can* be tracked right down to its impact at the cash register.

It's just that somewhere along the line, marketers lulled themselves into settling for creative excellence, awareness, popularity, production values, and awards—in place of cold, hard sales—as evidence of marketing success.

If marketers want to hang on to their budgets, they should track results to the penny. They should know which programs work, and be prepared to show the bean counters a cost benefit at any time. They should identify and prune failures without waiting for a sales downturn to mandate it. They should do so early and often, investing big dollars in a marketing effort only when it has proven its worth in the testing stage, with all indications that the results are projectable.

In short, marketers should *prove* their work. "To prove," by the way, means *to test.* To subject assumptions to scrutiny. To establish the worth of a proposition.[2]

This is a book on how to do just that. It's not about how to write a marketing plan or craft an ad campaign. It's a book about *proving* your marketing plan or ad campaign before you invest a bundle in it. It's about busting marketing myths, which are legion. It's about how to find out, up front, which tactics work for you—and which don't. It's about designing marketing so that you can tell when it's making money and then capitalize on it—and adjust or retire it when it isn't. All of which means it's about stacking the odds for marketing success *demonstrably* in your favor.

Moreover, this is a book about using your noggin in ways most marketing people—in fact, most people in general—haven't been trained to do. It's about applying critical thinking skills and the scientific method to marketing. It's about trading folklore for reality.

Prove It Before You Promote It is a plea for sanity in marketing.

Upon reviewing this manuscript, a friend pointed out that critical thinking and science are subject to error. He's right, but the observation is hardly damning. That science acknowledges its fallibility is one of its strengths. Every scientific conclusion remains open to challenge, testing, and new information. Thanks to that, it is no longer considered a scientific fact that the sun moves around the earth, even though long ago someone with authority said otherwise, and our senses are inclined to agree.

The antithesis of science is dogma. Dogma does not countenance challenge. Thus, despite sound evidence to the contrary, some people cling to a belief that aliens built the pyramids, that bats are blind, that the lunar landing was a hoax . . . or that their marketing campaign is working.

The potential for error isn't a problem. Failure to allow for it is always a problem.

Acknowledgments

You should have seen *Prove It Before You Promote It: How to Take the Guesswork Out of Marketing* before friends and family stepped in and saved me from myself.

Warm thanks go to Mike Cuno, Kyle Curtis, Justin Ethington, Mike Foster, Bill Hanifin, Mike Huber, Ty Kiisel, Lisa May, Steve Newton, Alan Overmoe, Brad Overmoe, Henry Romagosa, Dortha Wade, Tim Williams, and John Wright. These people generously provided in-depth suggestions and important corrections. I am also grateful to Tess Roach, who pruned the manuscript of myriad factual errors, typos, and other embarrassments, and to Christine Moore, whose painstaking editing made me look smarter than I really am. Other thanks go to Matt Holt, Jessica Campilango, and Kate Lindsay. Of course, errors that managed to survive are my fault, no one else's.

Big thanks go to my agent, Michael Ebeling, for patient and useful coaching, and for taking me on as an author in the first place.

For much-needed encouragement, painstaking proofing, useful suggestions and keeping the shop running while I researched and wrote, thanks go to the team at RESPONSE Prospecting & Loyalty Strategies: John Bradfield, Aubrey

Hicks, Scott Hubka, Paul Martin, Mark Martinez, Erin Mendenhall, Stacey Soldan, Joe Szymanski, and Jessica Trump. These are the folks who make our shop a success.

Above all, I owe thanks to my family: Rebecca Cuno, Jeff Cuno, Sasha McKissick, Scott Cuno, and Taylor Oxley.

About the Author

S teve Cuno is founder and chairman of The RESPONSE Agency, a nationally recognized direct response marketing firm headquartered in Salt Lake City, Utah. Steve is an internationally published marketing authority, an award-winning creative talent, and a popular speaker at business seminars, conventions, and universities.

INTRODUCTION
DEBUNKING MARKETING MYTHOLOGY

A minister once found himself at odds with three other ministers over a point of doctrine. The three argued that, since they were in agreement with one another, the odds of their being right were three to one in their favor. In desperation, the holdout looked heavenward and appealed for backup. "He's right," boomed a voice from the sky. After a moment, one of three said, "Well, it's still three to two."

The joke strikes a chord because it flies in the face of a logical fallacy we all pick up naturally and early in life called *Argument from Authority*. For kids, there is no surer clincher than "Mom says" or "Dad says." We don't outgrow this mentality. Even as adults, if someone with authority says something is true, we tend to think it must be. Hence we find humor in the counter-natural idea of rejecting what should be the ultimate voice of authority.

While growing up, we stumble upon instances in which our parents weren't always right (watching TV didn't make us go blind), but we remain susceptible to Argument from Authority. As I write, people are shelling out big time for a so-called immune-system booster that in reality boosts nothing but the marketer's bank account. Why so easily duped? Because it was "invented by a teacher" who supposedly wearied of catching every germ that rode into the classroom on her students. Never mind the fact that scientifically valid double-blind tests show the concoction to have no measurable effect. It was invented by a teacher, so it supposedly must work.

Marketing has no shortage of authorities from which its practitioners can argue. Many of today's accepted marketing practices are based on authorities like "the way we've always done things," "everyone knows this is how you do it," "it says in *Communication Arts*," or "David Ogilvy/Bill Bernbach/Bill Chiat/Alex Bogusky/Jim Collins said . . ."

The fact is, authority figures aren't always right. There is no reason not to submit established marketing practices, assumptions, and claims to testing and scrutiny, and there is no blasphemy in doing so. But for some reason, marketers by and large don't. Many simply set sail without bothering to question if the accepted course really does lead to the golden fleece—or if any fleece is even out there.

Before you can prove the value of your marketing, you're going to have to learn how to detect and debunk marketing mythology. There is an abundance of it, and it has gone largely unchallenged for decades. It has certainly been long enough.

1

WHAT ANY FOOL KNOWS

Y ou probably know that a ten-ton iron ball falls to earth at the same speed as a half-pound iron ball dropped from the same height. But in earlier times, most people "knew" that the heavier object would fall faster.

How they knew is instructive. Scientific questions in those days were not a matter of hypothesis and testing, but of philosophy. It was true that heavy objects fell faster than light ones, scholars reasoned, because any fool knew they did. Thus this pseudo-fact, canonized by none other than Aristotle himself, reigned for over a millennium.

To change things, it took a skeptic by the name of Galileo to say, and I paraphrase, "Oh yeah? Let's see." Then he did something revolutionary for his time: He devised a test. He took two iron balls, one considerably heavier than the other, climbed to the top of a tower (possibly the Leaning Tower of Pisa), and dropped them together.[1]

I'd like to tell you that from the moment the iron balls simultaneously reached the ground a new theory prevailed, but that's not what happened. Instead, for this and other groundbreaking findings—like proving the earth orbits the sun—Galileo ended up in big trouble with thought leaders of the day for daring to challenge prevailing beliefs.

And *that* is also instructive.

ENLIGHTENED AGE?

Today we have the scientific method, thanks to which we no longer believe that flies spontaneously generate from decaying meat, fresh air is bad for us, or the sun circles the earth.

But even in our so-called enlightened age, people still jump to unwarranted conclusions and cling to individual pet notions that fail to stand up to scrutiny. Or, rather, that would fail to stand up if anyone bothered to scrutinize. Witness the many savvy and successful people you know who consult their horoscopes before traveling or dating,[2] wear magnets to ward off arthritis,[3] believe that cold causes colds,[4] abstain from chocolate to prevent acne,[5] or wear a lucky hat when golfing.[6]

Do not try telling these people that their conclusions are unscientific, much less erroneous, unless you're in the mood for a long and fruitless argument. You'll find they don't much care what the evidence says. Or, that they counter with anecdotal "evidence." Or, that they become belligerent and defensive.

Millennia have passed since Galileo's experiment, but people still don't like it when you challenge what any fool knows.

NOT SO HARMLESS

With the possible exception of abstaining from chocolate, many unfounded beliefs are arguably harmless.

But some are not. It's one thing to wear a silly hat to improve your golf game. It's quite another to stake your company's advertising budget and possibly its future on an unproven campaign because your ad agency says the campaign is "truly creative," "stands out," "will get noticed," "takes a risk," "will be remembered," and "has CLIO Award potential," and because you've always heard that these are the qualities that make advertising successful.

Yet every day, CEOs, marketing VPs, and other corporate decision makers do just that. They commit huge marketing budgets to advertising with little more to recommend it than the ad agency's saying, "Trust us because we're the experts and we think this will work." But the fact is, most marketers—on both the client and the agency side—don't really know if their advertising is selling anything or not.

They may *think* they know. If sales are up, if they're proud of their campaign, if the advertising garners awards, if neighbors enjoy the ads, and, in the case of the few who conduct pre- and post-campaign research, if awareness has increased—many a marketer concludes that the advertising must be selling.

All it takes to call that conclusion into question is a bit of critical analysis. It's as simple as stepping back and saying, "Just a darn minute. What does the evidence *really* show?" And, for that matter, "What *really* constitutes evidence?" A sales increase could result from factors other than advertising. Pride in your campaign is nice but, as evidence goes, irrelevant. Awards aren't conclusive, since both effective and ineffective ads win them. Feedback from neighbors isn't statistically valid. And high awareness doesn't ensure marketing success. (Consider that failed products like Yugo, Edsel, and New Coke *still* enjoy high awareness.)

Sadly, one rarely encounters this kind of critical analysis in marketing. For one thing, marketers on both the client and agency side are often more interested in defending their work than in challenging it. For another, good critical thinking skills come neither easily nor naturally to people in general, let alone to marketers. Our hunter-gatherer environment shaped our minds to act, not to pause and question. The predilection kept us safe. Hunter-gatherers pausing to analyze whether a ferocious roar indicated a hungry lioness or a parrot with a sense of humor stood a lesser chance of survival than their peers who simply ran.

We changed our environment faster than our minds evolved to keep up. Despite living in a relatively lioness-free world, we are still predisposed to draw conclusions fast and take action. Thinking things through remains an option that most of us decline more often than we realize.

To be fair, the act-don't-analyze predisposition continues to serve us well fairly often in our modern world. That we need touch a hot burner only once to learn never to touch it again is a good thing. And there is often no harm when the predisposition happens to mislead us, as in the case of someone who decides that belching cures hiccups, because after several good belches the hiccups eventually subside.

But sometimes the predisposition misleads in costly ways. A seemingly harmless folk cure can result in serious consequences when chosen to the exclusion of a proven medical treatment. And marketers can waste big dollars by continuing to fund campaigns they believe to be effective when a critical look would reveal otherwise.

There are plenty of books on building marketing plans and writing ads. With *Prove It Before You Promote It: How to Take the Guesswork Out of Marketing*, my objective is the next step: subjecting cherished marketing practices to critical thinking and to the scientific method so as to discover and do more of what works, and avoid wasting money on what doesn't.

Expect a hue and cry from marketing and advertising people everywhere. Like carnival psychics who balk at testing because "the spirits won't cooperate when there's a skeptic in the room," many marketers will tell you their craft is an art, a gift that defies analysis. Just trust their creativity, they'll tell you, for true creativity produces sales as a matter of course in some ethereal, inexplicable way.[7] In so saying, they elevate marketing not just to an art, but to a form of magic. And amazingly, like marks who pay fortune-tellers for news of the departed, one business decision maker after another hands over the marketing budget. Tell them or their advertising agencies that award-winning creative work has not been proven to sell any better than non-award winners, and they will flatly deny it. Show them the numbers, and they'll disqualify them. Or, they'll counter with handpicked award winners that correlate with, but cannot be demonstrated to have caused, a sales increase.

But the inescapable fact is, if your marketing will work in the marketplace, it will stand up to valid testing. It follows that when marketing doesn't stand up to valid testing, you can be reasonably sure it won't work in the marketplace either, no matter how passionately you defend it, no matter how attached to it you may feel, and no matter how creative you find it to be.

Imagine how much more productive your marketing would become if you could set aside traditional notions of how to market, dismiss what gut intuition tells you, and instead test and evaluate a campaign—before you launch it—the way a scientist tests a hypothesis before proclaiming it law. Suppose you could prove successful campaigns in advance and then roll them out with confidence, while ferreting out unsuccessful ones and quietly retiring them without costing yourself and your company embarrassment or money.

Fortunately, for close to two centuries, there have always been a few renegades here and there who were willing to carefully test, measure, and observe the effects of their marketing. Chances are they didn't realize they were applying the scientific method to marketing and advertising, but that's exactly what they were doing. Their collective findings provide a vast body of knowledge about what does and doesn't work in marketing, most of which still applies. Successful marketing, they have repeatedly shown, isn't a question of opinion or taste, but of what can be consistently demonstrated to do a better job of leading more people to buy more often.[8, 9]

Another more recent, equally helpful effort has been gaining a good deal of momentum lately. I refer to a growing movement of modern scientist-writers who have dedicated themselves to debunking pseudoscience.[10] Fortunately, their work is increasing in popularity. (The success of the TV show *MythBusters* is a good example.) It turns out we marketers could learn a lot from them.

In the chapters that follow, I'll draw on insights from both camps, as well as on observations from my own experience with tested marketing. Chapter 2 tackles head-on one of the leading causes of untested, bad marketing decisions: the boss who makes idiotic marketing calls based solely on gut intuition. The chapter will balm the wounds

of any marketer who cringed at the sound of the boss saying, "My gut is never wrong." If this book shows up on
your chair anonymously bookmarked at Chapter 2, you are
said boss.

Chapter 3 draws upon psychology and statistics to reveal
common logical fallacies we all commit, why we commit
them, and how marketers are not immune. My hope is that
you will avoid making such leaps yourself. A particularly
beguiling leap—that of confusing correlation with causation—
is so disastrous for marketers that I committed the entirety
of Chapter 4 to it. This leads nicely into Chapter 5, wherein
the evidence soundly debunks the old advertising notion
that "true creativity" is all you need for a successful marketing campaign. In Chapter 6, I turn a critical eye on the legiti-
mate practice and rampant malpractice of branding. Critical,
but not cynical. I discard the branding hoopla bathwater, but
I rescue the baby with a look at the characteristics and power
of a rock-solid brand.

If those chapters fail to offend, Chapter 7 is sure to do the
trick. This is where I reveal why your favorite marketing
books may provide useful food for thought but should
never be accepted as blueprints for success. With few exceptions, marketing books are anecdotal, not scientific, and
are not reliable predictors of what works in the market.

Chapter 8 borrows from neurological and behavioral science to show why most predictive research is nothing of
the sort, whether qualitative or quantitative. But don't de-
spair. I'll rescue you in Chapter 9, where I show how to
conduct predictive research that's actually valid and
reliable.

Most of *Prove It Before You Promote It* starts with marketing
and subjects it to the rigors of scientific testing. Chapter 10
turns things around. It starts with scientific findings about

human behavior and then explores implications for marketing. Cognitive science, it turns out, can tell us much about why some marketing approaches seem to work better than others.

In Chapter 11, I show you how to map out a marketing strategy within which creativity can be properly nourished and disciplined.

Finally, with sound critical thinking and good science under our belts, we are ready in Chapter 12 to address the proper role of intuition in marketing. It turns out it really does have one.

Throughout *Prove It Before You Promote It*, I'll show you what people who measure marketing and advertising know, along with how they know it, so you can evaluate and even test their conclusions for yourself. I'll show you what science tells us about common errors in human thinking, how we unwittingly impose these errors upon marketing, and how to avoid doing so in the future. I'll share some of my own adventures from a career of subjecting marketing and advertising to the rigors of valid testing. I'll expose how selected, time-honored, universally accepted marketing practices fail to hold up in the face of critical thinking. And I'll invite you to empathize with me from time to time as I beat my head against the wall because of those who just don't get it.

Not that I intend to leave naught but destruction in my wake. In the process of debunking, I also reveal what all this tells us about doing marketing the smart way: scientifically and with projectable results.

My hope is that you'll emerge committed to marketing based on sound judgment and real evidence instead of marketing folklore. Perhaps you'll even become a debunker yourself. We could use a few more.

A word of warning: effecting change isn't easy. The more people invest themselves in a belief, the more likely they are to defend it, even in the face of facts proving the belief wrong. Psychologist Leon Festinger found that people who commit time and resources to provably erroneous beliefs— from investment schemes to UFOs—tend to remain resolute.[11] Rather than admit defeat, they prefer to disqualify the facts ("I lost money but the system works") or modify the original claim ("the aliens didn't visit Earth as predicted because the media were there"). It's all too human, it seems, to do anything but face facts when something we've pursued long and hard turns out to be unsupportable. Marketers aren't so different when it comes to letting go of cherished practices.

So don't expect the information you're about to pick up to make you many friends. It's good information, but it is largely overlooked—in fact, *disdained*—by well-respected marketing and advertising authorities who prefer to do things they way they've always done them. Prepare to ignore the mainstream while you go on to success. There's no need—or excuse—to bet the marketing budget on a whim or a hunch.

Critical thinking and the scientific method brought the rest of the world out of the Dark Ages a millennium ago. It's time marketing caught up.

SUMMARY POINTS FROM
WHAT ANY FOOL KNOWS

- People do not readily give up cherished beliefs, even when proven wrong.

(Continued)

- Betting a marketing budget on tradition constitutes an unwise and unnecessary risk.

- There is a vast body of knowledge about what works in marketing, thanks to over a century of scientifically tested marketing approaches. Marketers ignore it at their peril.

- Ongoing scientific discoveries about human behavior can provide useful information to marketers who care to read between the lines.

- Successful marketing isn't a question of opinion or taste but of what consistently leads more people to buy.

- You can use both critical thinking and the scientific method to improve marketing success and minimize loss.

- There's no need—or excuse—to bet the marketing budget on a whim or a hunch.

2

YOUR GUT DOESN'T KNOW SQUAT

Caution: a poorly made marketing decision is afoot.

Fingers on chin, the boss draws a portentous breath and says, "I'm going with my gut on this one." Then, to ensure no one questions the higher authority of the executive lower half, the boss adds, "And my gut"—pause for effect usually inserted here—"is never wrong." Thus, with no more evidence than gastrointestinal inclination, the boss embraces or dismisses a marketing proposal.

Most companies don't track marketing and advertising effectiveness, so by the time your boss turns out to be right or wrong, it's possible no one will be able to tell the difference. *But I can tell you right now that gut intuition is one of the worst ways out there for predicting the outcome of a proposed marketing campaign.* I'm not talking about experience based intuition, like detecting a poker player's *tell* or noticing that many people touch their nose before fibbing.[1] That's called "reading the clues," which I address later on. This chapter debunks the belief that intuition is some sort of ethereal, even magical gift for predicting—without testing—how people will react to your marketing. "I know my customers," your gut tells you, "and I know how they'll respond."

No, you don't. In fact, chances are you don't realize how often your gut (and everyone else's) is dead wrong.

GUT SUCCESS RATIOS

There would be nothing objectionable about gut-driven marketing if guts were always right. Or even usually right. They are neither.

At best, the ratio of correct to incorrect gut-driven decisions is 50-50.

Here's why. For every visionary's gut that turns out to be right, someone else's gut—which is also "never wrong"—necessarily turns out to be in error. Fred Smith's gut told him the nation would embrace an overnight courier like Federal Express, but his Yale professor's gut disagreed. George Martin's gut told him the world would love the Beatles, but the Decca record company's Dick Rowe responded with his now-infamous gut reaction, "Guitar bands are on their way out." Henry Ford's gut told him he would grow rich making automobiles that the average American family could afford, but his early partners' guts disagreed.[2]

I don't find 50 percent odds encouraging, but if you do, I must now tell you that your gut's odds are really much, much lower. The examples mentioned here are based on ventures that turned out to be successful. Consider the number that have bombed and those that continue to bomb every day: Edsel, New Coke, Yugo, rock bands that never make it, novels languishing on clearance tables, retail outlets and restaurants that close inside three months, movies no one goes to see, entrepreneurs who file for bankruptcy, products no one buys. More ideas flop than fly, yet behind every flop is a gut that assured a believing visionary, "It'll work." Add to that the fact that many of these gut decisions were backed by research and experience, and gut intuition begins to look more and more fallible.

But just a moment. What about all the intuitive judgments that correctly predicted the failure of an idea? Weren't they right most of the time? So isn't declining new ideas the safest approach of all?

In cases that actually went to trial in the marketplace, yes. And no. Killing all new ideas certainly ensures avoiding the failures, but it also ensures missing out on the occasional breakthrough moneymaker. Thus, Thomas Edison missed out by championing direct instead of alternating current; Henry Ford lost ground to competitors by refusing to offer a choice of models and colors; and the founders of Starbucks decided they'd rather sell their company than lower themselves to offering brewed coffee in addition to whole beans and grinders. Missing a great opportunity is risky in its own right.

Of course, most ideas never make it to market. Most are killed by someone's gut intuition in the conference room. Without a trial, there is no way of knowing just how many early-aborted plans might have turned out to be the Beatles. Or not.

YOUR GUT INTUITION ISN'T THE EXCEPTION

Even the guts of the best, most successful marketers are subject to randomness. They are right some of the time, and wrong some of the time.

In short, gut intuition is not reliable.

Now, you may believe your intuition is the exception. Perhaps by your own tally, your gut has proved right 90 percent of the time. In that case, I would say there are three possibilities. The first has to do with disqualification, the second with incomplete information, and the third with coins.

Disqualification is the very human tendency to embrace what confirms our suspicions and to overlook what contradicts them. People who say "you *always*..." or "you *never*..." commit this error. So do people who believe a correct prediction confirms a fortune-teller's power but an incorrect one means the spirits were uncooperative that day. People whose gut intuition seems right "most of the time" most likely forget or *disqualify* the times it was wrong.

Incomplete information is another problem. In many organizations, to tell the boss that his or her idea flopped is a career-limiting act—so all the boss ever hears is, "You were right again." And when the boss kills an idea, there's no opportunity to learn whether the idea would have worked. Information can fail to reach us even when no one deliberately suppresses it. If you believe your advertising is producing sales but no one can verify its actual effect at the cash register, you really don't know whether it's working or not. You just think you know.

But maybe, just *maybe*, your gut intuition *is* right most or even all of the time. Not all people who believe they have an infallible gut have counted wrong or are underinformed. They may simply be lucky coin flippers. In his book *Science Friction: Where the Known Meets the Unknown*, Michael Shermer observes, "If you conduct a coin-flipping experiment and record heads or tails, you will shortly encounter streaks. How many streaks and how long? On average and in the long run, you will flip five heads or tails in a row once in every thirty-two sequences of five tosses." It would be unusual for anyone's gut intuition to be right most of the time. But if yours really has been, you may be a rare beneficiary of randomness. Beware the next time you toss a coin.

READING THE CLUES

There is a fourth possibility behind the perception of oft-right gut intuition: that what's right from time to time turns out not to be your gut at all.

I worked my way through college selling shoes in a well-known department store. One day an attractive young woman and her friend graced my sales floor. Not a particularly adept flirt, I did what I could. I asked her to indulge me in a bit of fortune-telling. When she skeptically agreed, I told her what religion she belonged to. I was right, which surprised her. Then I told her that she was a musician. Right again. Then I said, "Now I'll tell you what your instrument is." After a moment, I said, "You're a singer." Her jaw dropped. So did her friend's. I had amazed them.

Fortunately, I didn't amaze myself, so I didn't buy a set of tarot cards and go into business as a fortune-teller. I knew I wasn't clairvoyant; I had relied on detection and a little bit of luck. As the attractive young woman paid for her shoes, I noted a religious symbol on a card in her wallet. Telling her she was a musician was mere fishing: a musician myself, I was looking for common ground. Having guessed right, I went on. When I promised to reveal what instrument she played, I saw her exchange a "now we have him" look with her friend. Ah, I realized, it's not an instrument per se. The only remaining possibility was that she was a vocalist.[3, 4]

As easily as I might have attributed divining my customer's religion, musical interest, and singing talent to clairvoyance, I might have credited gut intuition. In fact, over time, I might have decided my gut was pretty astute. After all, I have had my share of experience with correct discernment. But my gut didn't tell me when a teen from my neighborhood was lying; I learned his body language. My gut didn't tell me to decline a prospective client; the resemblance of his behavior to that of past bad clients did. My gut didn't tell me a strong offer would increase sales for a client; I knew the effect of offers from experience. Much as a gambler learns an opponent's *tell* through observation, I learned to read certain clues that consistently accompanied specific behaviors.

I hesitate to even bring up reading the clues, because I know some of you will say, "Fine. It's not my gut that's never wrong; I'm just uncannily good at reading clues. Whatever it is, call it gut or perceptiveness, it's never wrong." There are two problems with this conclusion. One is that it's hard to distinguish the gut that reads clues from the gut that entertains pure whimsy. Did your gut intuition tell you a job interview went well, were you attuned to the interviewer's positive responses, or were you oblivious to the clues and simply guessed right? The other is that reading clues is not a science and is subject to error. The brightest people misread clues (mental health experts who confuse pseudodementia, a symptom of depression, for Alzheimer's disease), fail to see clues (otherwise astute parents who are the last to learn their kids are on drugs), see clues that aren't really there (weapons of mass destruction in Iraq), and let ego mislead (male CEOs who think all the young women at the company party want to dance with them).

If you have enjoyed a certain amount of success reading clues, good for you. But don't bet your marketing budget on it.

I hope I have persuaded you to check your gut intuition at the marketing department door. But doing so begs the question, what exactly *should* you bet your marketing budget on? Aren't you in your position largely because of your skills, experience, and *judgment?*

But that's just it: No one is asking you to check your judgment at the door. On the contrary, I'm asking you to overrule your gut *in favor of* good judgment. Good judgment doesn't rely on supposition, jump to conclusions, accept anecdotes as proof, indulge superstition, act without reason, mistake correlation for causation, or stubbornly cling to the unsupportable. Good judgment seeks knowledge. It questions, researches, hypothesizes, experiments, observes, confirms, weighs, reconsiders, and tries again. Above all, good judgment remains ever willing to reevaluate, admit when it is wrong, right itself, and learn from successes and failures.

Admitting that your gut doesn't know squat is a good starting place on the road to critical thinking. If I've persuaded you to at least consider the possibility, a good next step is to learn how marketers unwittingly fool themselves on a regular basis, so you can avoid doing it to yourself. Let's look at some leaps.

SUMMARY POINTS FROM
YOUR GUT DOESN'T KNOW SQUAT

- For a number of reasons, most people don't realize how often their gut intuition is dead wrong.

- The odds do not favor gut intuition. In many cases, gut intuition has less than a 50 percent chance of being right.

- If you trust gut intuition more than evidence, you expose your marketing budget to unwise and unnecessary risks.

- It's not uncommon for luck, selection bias, and other factors to mislead people into believing their gut is right most of the time.

- As distinguished from gut intuition, you may be skilled at *reading clues*. Even this is not an exact science, and it has its risks.

- You do *not* intuitively know how your customers think or feel, or how they will react to your next marketing campaign.

- Admitting that your gut doesn't know squat is a good starting place on the road to critical thinking and successful predictive marketing.

- There are significant differences between gut intuition and good judgment. Fire the first and promote the second.

3

LEAPS

I n 1993, Erin Brockovich spearheaded a civil action against Pacific Gas & Electric, the predominant gas and electric utility in northern California. When an unusual number of cancer cases arose in and around Hinkley, California, Brockovich discovered that PG&E had been dumping the carcinogen hexavalent chromium into the water supply. PG&E's pollution was deemed responsible for the cancer, and the utility ended up paying $333 million in settlements.[1] I should add that, in 1993, $333 million was considered to be a lot of money.

That PG&E caused Hinkley's cancer is an easy leap. After all, it is a fact that PG&E polluted the water with hexavalent chromium, and it is a fact that hexavalent chromium is a carcinogen. But a leap it remains. A jury of scientists would rule that Brockovich failed to prove anything.

In *Science Friction*, Shermer explains, "Millions of Americans get cancer—they are not randomly distributed throughout the country; they are clustered." So are, he adds, incidents of water pollution. A map of the entire United States reveals polluted sites without cancer explosions, and cancer explosions not on polluted sites. Zero in on an area like Hinkley where the two happen to overlap, and you will see a strong correlation. Zero in on an area where they don't, and you'll see no correlation at all.

Before you dismiss this argument with, "Duh, we're talking about *a known carcinogen*," let's add one more piece of information. Hexavalent chromium is a carcinogen only when inhaled, not when mixed in water. The trace amount of the chemical in Hinkley's water, while certainly not an appealing recipe, was most likely harmless.[2]

A broader perspective weakens the geographic pollution-cancer correlation and, when considered along with the fact that hexavalent chromium is harmless in water, casts doubt on whether Brockovich stumbled upon a cancer cause or upon overlapping random events—and made a leap from there. Apparently, PG&E feared a jury of nonscientists would be likely to make a similar leap and settled out of court.

But it doesn't take a highly sensationalized, emotionally charged case like this one to lure intelligent people—including marketers[3]—into making questionable leaps.

Here are some common leaps marketers make every day to their own detriment. They (and anyone else) would do well to learn to recognize them so they do not fall prey.

MISTAKING AN ARGUMENT FOR PROOF

In grade school, we are trained to construct an *argument*. Open with an assertion. Back it up with evidence. Summarize and close. There. You've proved your point.

Except, you haven't. Otherwise, the following argument would constitute proof:

> *The earth doesn't spin on an axis. You can demonstrate this yourself. Try to stand still on a ball of any size spinning at any speed, and you will tumble off. Yet you can stand on the earth without falling, fighting for balance, or even feeling the slightest tremor. Therefore, the earth doesn't spin. When you see the sun cross the sky, it must be the sun that moves.*[4]

Marketing history is brimming with unfortunate decisions based on arguments that appeared sound when they were made. Nissan Motors introduced its Infiniti line with TV commercials that showed scenery instead of the car, based on the argument that not showing the car would heighten curiosity. Sony introduced its white portable PlayStation with a photo of a white woman grasping a black woman by the jaw, based on the argument that the approach would dramatize the contrast between the black and white products. Coke replaced its flagship formula, based on the argument that in taste tests people preferred the new recipe. However compelling those arguments seemed at the time, they all eventually proved wrong. Low sales forced Nissan to show the car after all, accusations of racism forced Sony to officially apologize for and pull the offending ads, and, as you probably know, consumer outrage forced Coke to bring back its original formula.

I once worked on a product introduction for a large software company whose management had grown full of themselves. They were bringing an inferior product to market late, but believed it would succeed because the company was the market leader—and because the marketing team had commissioned a commemorative music CD, by a composer of some celebrity, to promote it. With difficulty, I kept a straight face as I heard the executives convince one another with this argument: "The music is so beautiful, people will listen to it and want to buy our software." When the product bombed and the software publisher tumbled from its leadership position, a new argument emerged: "Our competitor treated us unfairly."[5]

No matter whom they convince, arguments are not proof.

ERGO PROPTER HOC

We humans are given to assuming that what happened first caused what happened next. We even honor this popular leap with its own Latin saying, *post hoc, ergo propter hoc*: "After this, therefore because of this."

Take, for instance, testosterone. Thanks to the strong correlation between aggressive behavior and testosterone levels, testosterone often gets the blame when people—especially men—end up fighting. This is patently unfair to testosterone, which surges only *after* an aggressive display.[6]

In marketing, as in biology, it's not unusual for what happened before to receive credit for what happened after, justified or not. And often it is not.

A look at the correlation between spending on advertising and winning an election provides a good example. A brilliant analysis by Steven D. Levitt and Stephen J. Dubner in their book, *Freakonomics: A Rogue Economist Explores the Hidden Side of Everything*, shows that candidates already favored to win are better able to raise funds and, therefore, spend more during a campaign. It appears that spending doesn't create the win as much as the looming win facilitates the spending.

Examined in that light, successful products with large advertising budgets beg the same chicken-and-egg question: Does the large ad spend make the product successful, or does the successful product command a larger ad budget? Without empirical data establishing causation, either or a combination of both may be true.

Once, a brand new client of my company, RESPONSE, informed us that we were required to feature her picture in every ad we produced for her company. It seems she had recently run two ads, one successful, one not, and the successful ad displayed her picture. The ads had other differences, ran in different publications, targeted different audiences and appeared at different times, but, according to her, all of that was beside the point. Her photo preceded success; therefore, it caused it.[7]

I doubt her reasoning persuaded you any more than it did me, but just in case, let's apply a little *reductio ad absurdum*—that is, take her argument to the extreme—and utterly expose the fallacy. When I was in the middle of a new business presentation, a rather unseemly growl moaned out from my abdominal region. I was embarrassed, but we won the business. A similar incident preceded winning another account not long after. Following her logic and in the spirit of *post hoc, ergo propter hoc*, I would seek to ensure that an unseemly intestinal noise interrupted every new business pitch.

With our ego's unwitting complicity, randomness can easily fool us into giving credit where it isn't due. Usually, conveniently, and not surprisingly, that means giving it to ourselves, but on occasion a ray of self-honesty shines through. The advertising agency business suffered for a time in the wake of September 11, 2001. Two years later, a business reporter asked agencies that managed not only to survive but to grow during that time to share their secret. In the resultant article, one agency credited their "superior creative product," another their "proprietary strategic methodology," and another their uncanny "ability to avoid the wrong kind of client." At these, I rolled my eyes. But I was impressed with the agency head who said, "I could list the things we did right, but I could also list some things we did wrong. Did our smart moves keep us in business, or did plain old luck save us despite our mistakes?"

What happens first doesn't necessarily bring about what happens next. For planning purposes, it's important to be able to differentiate a *cause* from mere randomness in one's favor—that is, luck, good fortune, or whatever you care to call it. Knowing the difference can keep us from subjecting the marketing budget to needless risk.

Besides, acknowledgement and gratitude for good fortune can help keep us grounded.[8] As marketers, and as people.

ANECDOTES AS CONCLUSIVE

Anecdotes can lead to good things. Native Americans had their stories about how chewing willow bark alleviated headache and fever. It turned out to be true and, in time, led to the development of aspirin.

But anecdotes can also lead to bad things. In seventeenth-century Salem, Massachusetts, anecdotes condemned 20 people to death by unspeakable torture for witchcraft. More recently in America, anecdotes from so-called Repressed Memory Syndrome demolished families, ruined reputations, and sent innocent people to jail.

The trouble with anecdotes is that no matter how conclusive they appear, they remain unverifiable stories and at best represent but isolated incidents. They must be received as such until they have been carefully tested and verified in a controlled environment. In *Science Friction*, Shermer quotes fellow scientist Frank Sulloway: "Anecdotes do not make a science. Ten anecdotes are no better than one, and a hundred anecdotes are no better than ten."

People find anecdotes compelling. Every marketer of miracle diets knows and exploits this fact with headlines like "I lost thirty pounds in six weeks!" The fact that the ads work despite "results not typical" in the fly-type tells you something about the power of anecdotes to persuade (not to mention the morals of marketers who trumpet misrepresentations and minimize facts). And marketers are as prone as anyone to being duped by anecdotes. When a funny campaign succeeds, marketers want their own funny campaigns. When a jingle takes hold, they suddenly need a jingle of their own. When a celebrity endorsement persuades, they scurry off in search of their own celebrities. Yet for every anecdote of a successful campaign using humor, a jingle, or a celebrity, there are anecdotes of failed campaigns using the same tactics. None of them prove anything.

I was once visited by a would-be entrepreneur who wanted to market small packages of belly button lint. (I'm not making this up.) She "knew" her product would be a hit because, after all, a few decades earlier the Pet Rock made someone a lot of money. True enough. But one anecdote, I explained, even in the form of the wildly successful Pet Rock, hardly constitutes precedent. More telling is the dearth of successful imitators in its wake.

Anecdotes can lead to launching bad campaigns, and they can also lead to killing good ones. When RESPONSE created a direct mail offer that outpulled the industry standard for that product by 350 percent, the client "heard" that "someone" had objected to our headline—and told us to discontinue the campaign.

Anecdotes raise possibilities. They never point to sure bets.

STEREOTYPING

Early in my career, I worked on a project for a company that sold services to the trucking industry. My myopic predecessor leaped to the conclusion that all trucking companies were run by mindless men who, at the mercy of their hormones, had only to be given a glimpse of cleavage before opening up their hearts and wallets. Sales were dismal. When I took over, I retired the buxom models and crafted advertising that focused on benefits. Sales took off.

My predecessor's campaign was an example of stereotyping. He misjudged trucking company decision makers as shallow, easily manipulated drones.[9] One can also err in the other direction, that is, stereotyping the market as too sophisticated to "fall for" techniques that work on everyone else. When RESPONSE was hired to recruit MBA students for a prestigious private college, faculty recoiled at our suggestion of rewarding applicants with a $25 gift card. They argued that such a premium was negligible against the $30,000 price tag of an MBA, did not align with the quality of student the school wished to attract, and would hurt the school's image. Finally, we reached a compromise. Half the mailing list received the $25 offer; half didn't. In the final count, the former outperformed the latter eight to one.[10]

There is a difference between stereotyping and profiling. Stereotyping is a leap to a prejudice-driven, preconceived notion. Profiling has to do with getting to know your customer, and it's a very smart thing to do. While auditioning potential actors for a commercial selling investment software, I explained to the hopeful actors and actresses that they would be appealing to men age 45 and over. One offended candidate reprimanded me with a reminder that women invest too. I conceded as much. But an analysis of who actually purchased and used this software showed that men liked it and, for reasons beyond us, women didn't. The Law of Least Resistance says you're a fool to try selling a product to people who don't want it, especially when people who *do* want it are right under your nose. So we targeted men.

It works both ways. When helping a client sell a lip-plumping product, we targeted women, even though there are men who use lip plumpers. Similarly, one should target women when selling health insurance to families. Notwithstanding that there are men involved in the family's health care, such decisions are largely driven by women. This is neither sexism nor stereotyping. It's targeting.

GOD OF THE GAPS

"God of the gaps" is the term scientists coined for the all-too-human practice of attributing what we cannot explain through direct observation to some sort of magic. We are loathe to say "I don't know" when there is a gap in our understanding of how the universe works. Instead we tend to chalk up what escapes us to spirits, gods, poltergeists, karma, the stars, or the ever-handy "it was meant to be."[11]

Defaulting to a god of the gaps to explain the not-yet-understood is tantamount to saying, "What I cannot understand must be beyond human understanding." It's healthy and wise to concede the limits of our imagination, but not to mistake that limit for a valid end point. There was a time when no one could imagine that diseases like schizophrenia and multiple personality disorder resulted from anything short of demonic possession. Fortunately for victims and their families, the medical profession didn't settle for what reigned for years as the only imaginable explanation.

Advertising's god of the gaps is none other than Creativity Itself. The argument goes like this: *When a product with Highly Creative advertising succeeds, it's because the advertising was Highly Creative. If the product fails, it would have failed even more miserably had the advertising not been Highly Creative. Either that, or there was some mix-up wherein we mistook a campaign for being Highly Creative but now we realize we were wrong. How do we know? Because Highly Creative advertising always works. It's in the gaps. (About those wildly successful products like Cascade dishwasher detergent whose advertising doesn't even register on the Creativity Scale? Flukes. All of them.)*[12]

There can be many reasons behind a product's success or failure. Without proper testing and controls, they are impossible to isolate and prove. But the inability to fathom more than the explanation at hand—whether it's creativity or any other—does not validate that explanation.

ALL OR NOTHING

I learned a thing or two about all-or-nothing dilemmas when I was 23 and just married. My new bride asked, "Do I look better than usual today?" Uncharacteristically, I took a moment to think before answering. Realizing that "yes" or "no" would be equally damning answers, I opted out of the all-or-nothing situation and said, "You always look great, though I can tell you've done something different today."[13]

All-or-nothing thinking assumes absolutes: it's either all A or all B, with nothing in between. It also assumes there's neither a C nor a D. As you can see, all-or-nothing thinking quickly and unjustly begins limiting your options—and your outlook.

Marketing is a great place to entrap ourselves with all-or-nothing thinking. I once met with a prospective client who was prepared to spend two million dollars per year on direct mail. One strategy my team suggested involved testing a double postcard that would fold to nine by six inches. Before I had a chance to explain what the postcard would *say* or how it would *look*, the prospect interrupted, "Get me a ruler and some paper." He proceeded to fold and tear the paper until he had a blank sheet in front of him folded to nine-by-six. "We mailed something that size once," he said. "Doesn't work." I politely explained that the size of the piece wasn't the entire strategy. We actually had plans to print some words and pictures on it that might differ from his earlier effort. No matter. They tried it once. Didn't work. All or nothing.

"Tried it once and it didn't work" comes up more often than you might expect. If you listen to enough marketers recount what they have tried *once*, all-or-nothing thinking can lead you to conclude that TV, direct mail, online marketing, catalogs, radio, and newspaper never work—notwithstanding the merchants of the world who have experienced otherwise.

What makes all-or-nothing thinking all the more damaging in marketing is that without proper testing and controls, marketers don't really know what it was about their advertising that made it succeed or fail. Was it the medium? The targeting? The schedule? The offer? The color? The font? The tone? The photo? The layout? The weather? "Tried it once" means you tried one combination of all of the above—once. Who knows what might have happened had you tried a few variations.

Nothing in marketing works or fails to work all of the time. What works in marketing is really a question of what options tend to be more effective than other options, over time, with sufficient consistency to ensure coming out ahead in the long haul. Note the words *tend to*. For every "tends to," there is an exception. Seminar registrations tend to plummet in July and rebound in September. Direct response TV spots tend to sell more from Friday through Monday, whereas direct response mail tends to sell more from Tuesday through Thursday. The random successful July (or poor September) seminar turnout, the successful direct response spot on Wednesday, and the successful mailer arriving on Saturday don't undo the trends. Do not let an exception needlessly usurp your rule.

SELF-SERVING RESEARCH

I appreciated what the TV network was trying to do. Management's commitment to nonviolent programming was laudable.

But their "research" was laughable. I sat in an auditorium with other ad agency people as a network representative presented the findings. The vast majority of people surveyed said they'd be more likely to patronize companies that advertised on a station with wholesome programming.

It was a prime example of self-serving research. Wittingly or unwittingly, the survey questions were fashioned to produce answers the network wanted. What would anyone *expect* interviewees to say? "Actually, I'm an irresponsible person who prefers exposing my children to violence, wanton sex, suffering, and cruelty." Right.[14]

Moreover, this self-serving research didn't change the very important fact that competing networks delivered more viewers, spending aplenty, to their advertisers.

If you research to confirm what you already believe, you will find what you're looking for. Trouble is, unless you were lucky enough to start out with a good hunch, you will end up nowhere nearer the truth.

We tested a new direct mail package against the control package we created earlier for one of our RESPONSE clients. When results came in, the client told us that the control outsold the test two-to-one. Some time later, I learned that the marketing manager, who insisted on handling the printing and mailing process without our help, mailed four control packages for every one test package, and compared total responses instead of responses as a percentage of the total mailed. About now it probably won't surprise you to learn that the manager disliked the test version and favored the control. The manager arrived at the outcome he wanted by looking only at gross numbers. The moment response was adjusted relative to the quantities mailed, it became clear that it was the test package that outperformed.

The point of research should be to reveal answers. When marketers embark on research to reinforce or defend rather than discover, there is a danger of compromising the integrity and usefulness of the results.

SNEAKY BIASES

I use the term *sneaky* to give marketers the benefit of the doubt. Sometimes marketers honestly don't know the extent to which personal bias can sneak up and lead to amazing leaps.

Not that all bias is bad. A certain amount of healthy bias is good—it keeps us from wasting valuable time testing *every* hunch. In his engrossing book, *Discarded Science*, John Grant says, "... [S]cientists have limited amounts of time they can spend dissecting each and every new hypothesis that to them is quite patently nonsense." The same holds true with marketers. When a junior staff member rushes into your office and suggests promoting that new line of facial tissue with the headline "High Abrasion for Better Hygiene," it's okay to allow personal bias to kill the idea.

That said, here are common biases, which aren't quite so okay, that sneak up on the best of us.

Self-delusion. It's human to want to think well of ourselves, but the tendency can trip us up. Self-delusion is manifest when marketing managers say things like, "Our customers will pay more for our services because we're local and they'd rather not give their dollars to an out-of-state firm that charges less for the same thing." It is manifest in the company that inverts its organizational chart, putting employees on top and the CEO on the bottom ("I really believe that's true," says the CEO with wide-eyed sincerity), when every employee knows otherwise. It is manifest when a Hollywood film marketer complains to *Advertising Age* in 2006 that movie attendance is down because TV is losing its power as a medium for marketing movies; it couldn't possibly be due to the fact that Hollywood keeps turning out movies like *Snakes on a Plane.*

Selection bias. Each winter when I toss road salt on the driveway, it doesn't spread evenly. It lands in clumps. If I divide my driveway into three-foot-square areas, I'll likely find a square in which the road salt has landed most heavily and in which there are oil stains. From that I could conclude that oil stains attract road salt. Or I could admit I was guilty of selection bias by narrowing in on too small an area, and eliminating too many others, to draw reliable conclusions.

I once participated in a marketing program that failed. Clearly failed. Its purpose was to produce sales, and it

produced but a handful. I recommended that the client discontinue the campaign. But another party who happened
to be married to the project began selecting bits and pieces
of data to show favorable results. Here were two highly
affluent people who bought. Here were three long-term
customers who bought. Here was someone who spent more
than the average. By cherry-picking isolated bits of data, he
convinced the client that a failed program had actually
worked. This is like declaring an endangered species safe
upon locating a few specimens living in the wild, rejecting
global warming because you had to shovel snow last winter,
or proclaiming a dying forest in good shape because a few
selected trees seem to be thriving.

I once worked with the parent company of a not-for-
profit hospital. The hospital feared that letting the public
know that it was part of a larger conglomerate might
endanger donations. Focus groups ensued.[15] One participant
after another expressed no dismay over the hospital's ownership. The subject of contributions didn't even come up—
until, toward the end of the last group, one person, upon
prompting by the moderator, said, "I might be less inclined
to give to the hospital." The marketing manager seized that
single comment and parlayed it into "proof" that the hospital should distance itself from its ownership.

For the outcome you want, start with what you want
to prove and select the data that support it. But for more
reliable results, start with good data and see where they
lead you.

Starting with a predetermined conclusion (confirmation bias).
My friend Lynn was convinced of his own unpopularity.
To prove it, he fixed his eyes on his own feet and walked
past a group of people who knew him. When no one
greeted him, Lynn considered his point proved. He failed

to consider that his body language had made him un-approachable. The very nature of his "experiment" en-sured he'd end up with the outcome he wanted.

I worked for an agency that created two ads for a computer games company. The company disliked both ads, but agreed to test them. Other than the featured game, the ads were identical. One ad sold like crazy; the other flopped. The client concluded that the unsuccessful ad confirmed that both ads were bad. To the client, the un-successful ad proved the agency's work was weak, while the successful ad indicated a strong product. To our crea-tive director, it was the opposite: the successful ad proved the agency's work was great, while the unsuccessful ad indicated a weak product. Same data, different agendas, different conclusions.[16]

Hindsight bias. When, after the fact, you realize you "knew it was coming," it's possible you're being taken in by hindsight bias.

"I had a feeling he shouldn't be climbing that tree," says the parent to the physician casting a child's leg. "My dog knew an earthquake was coming," says the earthquake survivor upon recalling that, before the quake, Fido acted "kind of funny." "You should have known I wanted my salad dressing on the side," says the irrational diner, abus-ing the poor server who can't read minds.

Hindsight bias can wreak havoc in marketing. It can rob successes of their due with seemingly innocuous declara-tions like, "I knew it would work," "It was suggested many times before," or "Anyone could have thought of that idea." It can also enable blaming. After a disastrous campaign for which everyone had high hopes, it's all too human, easy, and common to castigate those who "should have known it wouldn't work."

INVENTING THE OBJECTIVE AFTER THE FACT

The marketing team of a medical products company proudly showed me their newest low-budget video and asked me what I thought. I asked what its objective was. "To sell the product," they said. I pointed out ways it might be strengthened toward that end. "Actually," they defended, "its purpose isn't so much to sell the product. It's more of an educational piece." I pointed out some ways it might educate better. They said, "It's not really meant to educate. It's meant to let people know we're here." At that point, I decided to keep quiet.

The practice of redefining objectives post-campaign is alive and well—and counterproductive—in marketing. I watched a company execute an expensive campaign whose stated purpose was to generate new business. When the dust settled, no new business had been won. So you can imagine my surprise when I heard the marketing manager who championed the campaign proclaim it a success "because it forced our people out of their offices to meet prospects face to face." Fine. Except that wasn't the original objective.

I met with a group whose mission was to promote tourism. The marketing manager showed me an ad they ran in national publications, and told me its objective was to generate information requests from prospective tourists. When I asked how the ad performed, the ad manager admitted that the volume of requests was disappointing. "But," the ad manager added, "The ad stopped people and made them look at it, so it did its job." Funny. *Before* the ad ran, the ad's objective was to generate inquiries. *After* the ad ran, its objective conveniently morphed into making people stop and look.

Setting or changing your objective to accommodate the results of an already executed campaign is like throwing a dart and then drawing a bull's-eye around it. You may convince yourself that you never miss, but you won't win very much beer.

ASSUMING CORRELATION MEANS CAUSATION

In his excellent book, *The Demon-Haunted World: Science as a Candle in the Dark*, Carl Sagan offers this example of confusing correlation with causation: "A survey shows that more college graduates are homosexual than those with lesser education; therefore, education makes people gay."

That is, of course, an easy one to see through, but not all assumptions of causation are so easily debunked. Consider the number of people who, despite debunking, still believe that immunizations cause autism, based on a correlation between increased autism diagnoses and the dawn of immunizations, along with a correlation between the typical age at which autism symptoms appear and the age at which vaccinations are administered. There is no evidence that immunizations are responsible for a rise in autism—or, for that matter, that a rise has even occurred—but, as with Erin Brockovich and the PG&E case, this is an emotionally charged topic not easily settled with a few words of logic.[17]

Correlation versus causation is a no less emotionally charged issue among marketers. It is a big subject that deserves its own chapter. Fortunately, it happens to be next.

SUMMARY POINTS FROM *LEAPS*

- Marketers are not immune to cognitive leaps.

- A good argument does not constitute proof.

- What happens first doesn't necessarily cause what happens next.

- Anecdotes, no matter how compelling, are not proof.

- It is important not to confuse *stereotyping*, which promotes injustice, with the viable marketing practice of sound *targeting*.

- There is no justification for invoking magic as the only explanation for a phenomenon you cannot explain at the moment.

- All-or-nothing thinking is a form of small-mindedness that can keep you from discovering the right possibility.

- When the purpose of research is to confirm what you already believe, it isn't research.

- Not all bias is bad, but much of it is. You'd be surprised at how easily biases sneak up on you. No, you're not immune.

- Inventing an objective after the test will only mislead you.

- Finding a correlation, even a valid one, doesn't mean you've found a cause.

4

BEGUILED BY CORRELATION

Much of our early survival as a species depended on our ability to detect and capitalize on correlations. Linking fresh tracks with nearby game had much to do with our success in obtaining a meal. Linking crocodile eyes peering from the water with the sudden and unseemly deaths of fellow tribe members had much to do with our ability to avoid *becoming* a meal.

But being attuned to correlations has its downside. We can be fooled into seeing correlations where they're not. And where correlations do exist, we can be fooled into inferring significance that isn't there. Both of these are costly mistakes for marketers playing with big budgets.

ONCE IS NOT A CORRELATION

No matter how dramatic and seemingly unlikely, a one-time convergence of events does not make a correlation. At best, it makes a coincidence.

When I lived in Reno, Nevada, I had a visitor who wanted nothing more than to see a Nevada casino. So one warm day I drove him to Virginia Street, where we spent more time than I cared to, watching people feed quarters to one-armed bandits. As we made our way through the crowds, my friend bumped a woman's arm as she was pulling a slot-machine handle. Out poured a jackpot. Delighted, the player entreated him to remain and bump her arm with every subsequent pull.

Now that's just plain silly, isn't it? A one-time coincidence does not a correlation make, yet marketers often commit this thinking error. It's not unusual to encounter seasoned marketers who decide that a one-page employee manual giving salespeople discretion is the key to success because it seems to work for Nordstrom. Or who see Nike's success and decide to run ads featuring large photos with no copy and naught but an undersized logo all but hidden away in a corner. Or who find themselves unwittingly humming the American Family Insurance jingle and thus decide their product needs a jingle of its own.

Perhaps no one is better at jumping on the one-time success story than Hollywood. Movie producers seem particularly prone to deciding that a single successful film constitutes grounds for a genre. After the success of the early James Bond films came myriad, quickly forgotten spy movies. *Star Wars* launched lackluster knockoff space operas; *E.T.* prompted a spate of dismal failures about kids making friends with aliens; and *Indiana Jones* imitators like Richard Chamberlain as Allan Quatermain fell equally flat.

Reliable conclusions cannot be drawn from a limited convergence of events, no matter how unlikely the coincidence may appear. Otherwise, we might reasonably conclude that the sure way to boost sagging soda-pop sales is to abandon and then restore the original formula, that the way to win a presidential election bid is to lie in an attempt to cover up a past affair, that the way to end up with your own movie production company is to hop up and down on Oprah's couch shouting "I'm in love," and that the way to increase the loyalty of fans and strengthen a formidable marketing empire is to spend a few months in jail for securities fraud.[1]

A handful of coincidences are no more useful than one. If you studied Wendy's before the passing of Dave Thomas, you might decide that the secret to good marketing is to make a celebrity out of your CEO. You'd have Disney Productions, Southwest Airlines, Chrysler in the Iacocca days, and Oreck to back you up. But you'd also have to ignore all the companies that *failed* with a CEO spokesperson (like, among others, Chrysler in the Dr. Z days), not to mention all the companies that succeeded *without* using a CEO as a spokesperson.

CORRELATION MYTHOLOGY

Our attunement to patterns also leaves us prey to supposed correlations that may sound reasonable but are in fact nothing but myths.

You have probably heard how, during periods of overpopulation, tens of thousands of lemmings rush to an icy death in the Arctic Ocean. The correlation seems to demonstrate that nature has found a cruel way to hold down the lemming population.

You probably know about the correlation between red cars and speeding tickets, too. Red cars get more tickets, presumably because they call undue attention to themselves.

And if you've spoken with some obstetricians or maternity ward nurses lately, you probably know about the correlation between births and lunar phases. More babies are born under a full moon than during any other lunar phase.

There's just one problem. These are all myths. There is no such thing as mass lemming suicide;[2] red cars earn no more speeding tickets than cars of any other color;[3] and births are randomly distributed among all lunar phases.[4]

Yet these myths are widely accepted, and not just by the ignorant. Now, maybe the first two examples aren't fair. Few of us have had a chance to travel north and watch lemmings in action or to count speeding tickets by color of car. But look at the Full Moon/More Births myth. Its defenders are obstetricians and maternity ward nurses. These are people who receive training in science and critical thinking, and who have an opportunity to track the phenomenon for themselves. And yet they are fooled.

It's a sobering thought for us marketers, especially given that most of us were *never* schooled in science or critical thinking. Can marketers be fooled into swallowing correlation myths? It turns out the answer is an unequivocal *yes*.

In 1957, marketing researcher James Vicary announced the results of an experiment in which he spliced subliminal messages into the movie *Picnic* at a Fort Lee, New Jersey, movie theater. Every five seconds, "Drink Cola-Cola" or "Hungry? Eat popcorn" appeared for 1/3,000th of a second—allegedly too fast for viewers to notice with their conscious minds, but, also allegedly, not too fast to have subliminal impact. Vicary reported that during the six-week test Coke sales rose 18.1 percent. Popcorn sales, he said, rose 57.7 percent. The study is still used today to warn about the dangers of subliminal messages. There's just one problem. Vicary made the whole thing up.[5] Yet the myth persists among marketers and consumers alike.

Ever heard that no one reads long ads? Not true. I've personally disproved that myth many, many times on my own, and I'm not the only one to have done so. Those long (and admittedly ugly) ads crammed with type that appear month after month in in-flight and other magazines are some of the nation's top producers of cold, hard sales.[6,7]

Ever heard that no one really watches late-night TV and for sure no one with money dials those 800 numbers? We increased sales of natural gas fireplaces—not exactly a product for the poverty-stricken—tenfold when we moved the spot to late night. In fact, the very reason you see 800-number spots late at night is that they consistently pull more sales then than during prime time.[8]

Ever heard that stating a benefit in plain English, instead of couching it in cleverness, won't produce sales? While it's important not to mistake dull for clear, clarity always produces better results than trying to dazzle with puns and clever twists of phrase. Billions of dollars in household products are sold each day on afternoon TV with direct, straightforward, this-is-what-the-product-does formats, such as Lysol's "Disinfect to Protect," Pledge's "removes allergens while you dust," and Jet-Dry's "faster drying for a sparkling shine."[9]

Ever heard that putting *you* in a headline increases sales? The fact is, adding a healthy dose of *you* won't help a boring or irrelevant ad. Too little *you* won't hurt a brilliant ad. Although word changes have been known to make dramatic differences in ad performance (as advertising legend John Caples demonstrated more than once), one-word tricks are no match for solid strategy and compelling benefits.

With the abundance of marketing lore, discerning fact from fiction is a challenge. The best protection is to develop a good sense of critical thinking. Like Galileo, marketers are well advised to step back from the prevailing wisdom and ask, "Oh yeah?" It's also a good idea to check the evidence, its source, the test methodology, and just how conclusions were reached. And, if need be, test anew and monitor the evidence for yourself.[10]

CORRELATIONS WITHOUT A CAUSE

In its simplest terms, you have a correlation when you identify two or more consistently coinciding events.

Bird migration correlates with seasonal change. Lung cancer correlates with cigarette smoking. Tennis elbow correlates with playing lots of tennis. Picking fights with a wasp nest correlates with speedily finding yourself in pain.

But not all correlations are created equal. A correlation becomes useful only when there also happens to be *causation* involved.

Unfortunately, causation *isn't* always involved. In his book, *The Vision of the Anointed: Self-Congratulation as a Basis for Social Policy*, Thomas Sowell writes, "One of the first things taught in introductory statistics textbooks is that correlation is not causation. It is also one of the first things forgotten."

Remembering that correlation doesn't ensure causation is easier said than done. If after painting the cave wall we have a few good hunts, somehow we *know* that painting buffalo murals works magic upon our spears and prey. We learn that a high percentage of violent teenagers consume violent media, and we *know* it was the video games like Warcraft and counterculture icons like Marilyn Manson that turned those gentle teens into fiends. If enough seminar attendees walk barefoot over a bed of hot coals, we *know* that people can do anything they want *if they really believe they can.*

Here's the rub. While each of these cases actually represents a valid correlation, we trip ourselves up when we assume that by finding the correlation we have also found the cause. Cave paintings don't work magic on spears or buffalo.[11] Violent entertainment doesn't make monsters out of teens.[12] And motivational speakers don't inspire people to positive-think their feet into a fireproof state.[13]

Once we stumble upon a correlation, it's surprisingly easy to infer a cause that's simply wrong. One of our clients rigged an electronic bell to his company's front door. While he was at it, he decided to rig the bell to the back door, too, so that the bell sounded when either door opened. One morning, my client found an employee standing dead still in the reception area. The bell rang—triggered, unbeknownst to her, by the back door—and she hurried to another spot and froze. The bell rang again, and she moved and froze again. At length, my client asked what was going on. "I'm trying to see if the motion detector has a blind spot," she said.

The employee was unaware that use of the back door could sound the bell. She was also unaware that the door itself, not a motion detector, was the triggering device. On that particular morning when she visited the reception area, she noticed that the bell happened to ring when she moved. She quite reasonably assumed her motion was the cause and decided to experiment. As luck would have it, things were busy in the back that day. Each time she moved, the bell rang. Or, at least, so it seemed.

My client hires bright people, and this employee was no exception. Yet random chance fooled her into seeing causation where there was only correlation.

In marketing, it is equally easy, and not at all unusual, to infer cause where none really exists.

A public transit company hired our agency to create a direct mail campaign with the objective of increasing the number of riders. No sooner had we completed our work than the number of riders shot dramatically up. Transit company management received recognition for having met aggressive goals.

If I ended the story there, you might reasonably conclude that our stellar creative work did the trick. So let me add some details.

For one thing, this happened in the fall of 2005. Hurricanes had just devastated the Gulf Coast, wiping out major oil refineries there. Gas prices rose, and commuters all over America began leaving their cars at home and hopping on public transit instead. For another, when rides went up, the client withdrew the work assignment they'd given us. The campaign never made it off our designer's desk.

Okay, I admit to not playing fair when, up front, I left out that detail about the campaign's never having seen the light of day. Here are some more cases, but without the tomfoolery.

In his book, *Selling the Invisible: A Field Guide to Modern Marketing*, author Harry Beckwith avers that Bill Clinton won his first presidential election by switching focus midstream to the economy. Indeed, Clinton's campaign did take off at about the time of the switch. The more he talked about the economy, the more he gained in the polls. Definitely a correlation. Were I the adviser behind the strategic switch, I'd heartily endorse Beckwith's conclusion that it caused the turnaround.

But were I a scientist, I wouldn't be so sure.[14]

How do we *know* that focusing on the economy made the difference for Clinton? About that time, Clinton also played the sax on a popular late-night TV show. Perhaps *that* did it. Or, perhaps breaking news of his affair with Gennifer Flowers made him sexier to voters. Maybe it was something far more mundane. Perhaps the country had simply grown weary of George H. W. Bush. With a little imagination, it wouldn't be hard to suggest other possible causes as well.

Without test and control groups—all but impossible in a general election—we'll never know. All that remains is what we choose to believe. Not surprisingly, what we choose to believe has a lot to do with individual perspective.

Beckwith also tells a tale of Edelman and ACI, two telemarketing companies that opened within three months of each other. Edelman advertised heavily. ACI offered better technology but advertised less. Today, Edelman leads by a wide margin, and Beckwith alleges that its advertising made the difference.

Perhaps. But perhaps Edelman had more skilled presenters. Maybe being located in Omaha gave advantages to Edelman that being in Minneapolis didn't give to ACI. Maybe Edelman's three-month head start made a crucial difference. Maybe ACI's senior management forgot to read *Dress for Success*.

The fact is, Beckwith doesn't know why one company did better than the other, and neither do we. Beckwith is an ad agency guy, so naturally he'll want to assume that advertising made the difference. An ad agency guy myself, I'd like to make that assumption, too. But if the facts to justify the leap are there, Beckwith's book doesn't supply them.

I was acquainted years ago with an ad agency that ran a campaign for its savings and loan client. (That it was indeed a savings and loan tells you just how long ago this conversation took place.) The campaign compared choosing to open a money market account with this particular institution to betting on a winning race horse. When I expressed concern about a gambling analogy promoting a federally insured savings account, the creative director responded that deposits were up. "It's because of the ads," he said. That deposits were up was verifiable, but that the ads were responsible wasn't. The increase in deposits may as well have been caused by economic demand, an aggressive cross-selling program, generous incentives, happenstance, or a combination of these factors. Cause must be *established*, not *assumed*. Otherwise, when the savings and loan industry collapsed a few years later, it would have been equally valid to say, "It's because of the ads." Oddly enough, I don't recall hearing the creative director make that claim.

It's surprising how often we draw conclusions of causality that we're in no position to draw. If you give your best customers a punch card entitling them to one freebie for every 10 purchases, you may see a correlation between card-carrying customers and sales. But what you won't know is what's causing what. Are the cards causing the sales, or are the customers who already did most of the buying simply carrying cards now?

If you find that more people buy your product in one store than in another, you have a correlation. But *why* are sales higher in one store than another? The correlation may be tied to store preference, to in-store product placement, to the presence of competing products, to parking, or to myriad other variables. You'll need to dig deeper if you want to find and capitalize on the real cause.

AH, CAUSATION!

Why matters.

To illustrate, let's start with stomach ulcers.

For decades, doctors knew there was a correlation between stress and ulcers. After all, every person who developed an ulcer admitted to being under stress.

But there is a problem with that particular correlation. Name one adult who *isn't* under stress, and I'll show you a corpse. Linking ulcers with stress is like linking ulcers with people. Not very helpful.

In the 1980s, Dr. Barry Marshall, a resident physician in Australia, stumbled upon an additional correlation: Every stomach ulcer he examined was teeming with a bacterium called *Helicobacter pylori.*

When he wondered aloud whether *Helicobacter pylori* might be the real cause of ulcers, the medical profession lost no time disqualifying his finding. Not content to drop the issue, Marshall did the extreme. He swallowed a vial of *Helicobacter pylori*—and developed ulcers himself. Then, he successfully treated them with antibiotics. Today, it's accepted medical practice to treat ulcers with antibiotics in place of inflicting sufferers with needless, dangerous, painful surgeries. In Marshall's case, correlation indeed pointed to the cause—even though the earlier so-called correlation between ulcers and stress didn't.

Correlation can provide a great starting point. But when you can get to the cause, you have the beginnings of a solid foundation upon which to build solutions.

GETTING TO THE CAUSE IN MARKETING

Here's a useful tidbit if you happen to be a U.S. retailer: Most of your customers will wander to their right when they enter your store. In this case, one might argue that *why* doesn't matter as much as *what*. As long as the behavior is consistent, you can place must-see items to the right and increase their chance of being spotted by newly arriving customers. Who cares why?

But humor me for a moment. Take a guess. *Why* do people turn right? Most people to whom I put this question guess it has to do with how many people are righthanded. Indeed, most people *are* righthanded, so there we have a correlation. But what if I told you that in England, New Zealand, and the Bahamas, most people turn *left* upon entering a store? The correlation between being righthanded and turning right exists only in countries where people *drive* on the right. Globally, the way people turn upon entering a store correlates not with which hand they use to eat or write but with the side of the road they drive on.

So you might fare quite well not understanding *why* people turn to the right if your stores are in Michigan. But knowing what causes people to turn one way or the other can spare you substantial lost opportunity cost if you do business in countries where people drive on the left.[15]

Getting to the cause can be tricky, thanks to confirmation bias—the very human tendency to wring from the facts support for what we want to believe, regardless of where the evidence might otherwise logically lead. Conspiracy theorists provide an extreme example when they interpret a *lack* of evidence for their position as indicative of a cover-up and, therefore, evidence *for* their position. So do marketers who, rather than learn what works, prefer to justify their strategies by invoking an authority known as The Way We've Always Done Things.

I worked with a seasoned advertising manager who ran an awful promotional campaign. The headline and photo dominating the page had nothing to do with the selling message, which was hidden deep in the copy from all but the most determined reader. Though arguably creative, the ad simply required too much work on the part of readers to decipher it. Sales were dismal. After weeks of no results, the ad manager's CEO demanded the addition of a clear, benefit-oriented headline. Sales took off immediately, but the advertising manager didn't believe that the headline had made the difference. "My boss," he later told me, "doesn't understand that a campaign needs a few weeks to get a foothold. The headline change didn't make the difference. It was that people had to see the ad for a few weeks before they'd begin to respond."

In the absence of strict testing and controls, scientific integrity demands the admission that I can't conclusively say which one of them was right. But based on my experience with testing obscure against straightforward advertising, I am reasonably sure that this ad manager allowed his personal stake to bias his conclusion. In so doing, he missed an opportunity to find out *why* one ad version outperformed the other, and a greater, future opportunity to repeat tactics that work and retire those that don't.

In a series of tests for a client who owns a group of dry cleaning stores, we found that coupons offering a 50 percent discount outperformed coupons offering a premium hot cocoa mix. With hindsight bias, you might think it obvious that a hot cocoa offer would be less successful, but in advance of testing, offer performance can be hard to predict. (For instance, we dramatically increased orders for a business forms printer by offering buyers, most of whom were male, Victoria's Secret gift cards. Who'd have thought?) In any case, it certainly didn't help when, on the March day in the locale where our offer arrived in the mail, heretofore uncomfortably chilly temperatures gave way to uncomfortably warm ones.

So we shelved the cocoa and tested the 50-percent-off coupon against a 25-percent-off coupon. For the next three weeks, our client redeemed a considerable number of 25-percent-off coupons. To our surprise, few 50-percent-off coupons showed up. We had a *correlation*—more lower-value coupons were redeemed—but what was the *cause?* Our best guess, at that point, was that a 50 percent discount seemed too good to be true.

But something interesting happened at the end of the fourth week. Our client was deluged in 50-percent-off coupons. That was when the *why* became clear. The coupons had a one-month expiration date. People receiving the 25 percent offer responded promptly, but those receiving the 50 percent offer hoarded their cleaning right up to the expiration date.

More interesting and useful information followed. Though the 50-percent-off coupon brought in a sizably greater number of customers overall, post-analysis revealed that people who redeemed the 25-percent-off coupon converted at a higher rate to regular, profitable customers—which was the ultimate objective. Although the larger discount produced greater response, the smaller discount created more customers and more profit.[16]

This was a clear case where getting to the *why* helped us identify the more successful campaign for finding and growing customers, as distinguished from the campaign that simply correlated with the highest redemption rate.

WORTHY CAUSES

Here are some other correlations-with-causes that may interest you. Most of these have been tested and retested by direct marketers over the years and have been further confirmed with testing we have performed for our clients at RESPONSE. I'll note other sources when they apply.

- Shoppers spend more time at displays with plenty of room around them, away from high-traffic areas. That's because they don't like to pause where they're likely to be bumped by other shoppers.

- Long lines at the cash register of an otherwise empty store can induce would-be shoppers to leave.

- Diners have greater confidence in servers who write, rather than memorize, orders.[17]

- More people will leave a TV show to dial a toll-free number in the afternoon, late at night, and on weekends than during prime time. The reason appears to be that "fringe time" shows are less involving. People won't mind missing some of the show to make a call.

- Long copy outsells short copy.

- The part of a marketing letter that is read first and most often is the P.S. That's because readers tend to look to see who signed the letter; the eyes move down from there.

- On order forms, you will increase response if you include a little box for people to mark with a check. Be sure the box is square and empty—no fill color—and has no drop shadow.

- The best month of the year to sell personal improvement products is January because people still make New Year's resolutions.[18]

- Phone numbers should be large enough for a reader to spot without trying—which means it should be large enough to make your art director squirm. Placing an icon of a telephone next to the number will increase calls.

- A valuable free incentive offer will increase immediate response from consumers and business customers.

- The higher the income and education levels of your target market, the more effective a compelling incentive offer becomes.

- When generating business-to-business leads, it's not unusual for an incentive unrelated to what's for sale to outperform a more relevant incentive. Leads generated by unrelated incentives may be of lesser quality, but that can be offset by the larger volume of response.

- Subheadings and indented paragraphs increase readership because they break up and organize copy, making it more accessible to the reader.

- A sales letter in an envelope outsells a self-mailed sales brochure that has the same content.

- More people respond to direct mail midweek, but more respond to TV on weekends.

- The best day for e-mail response never stays in one spot for long: When e-marketers learn which day works best, they pour it on and drive the weary target market to respond better on other days.

- On the web, more people click on red buttons than other colors.

- More people click on buttons with clear instructions like "Click here to contact us" than buttons that merely say "Contact us."[19]

I ALMOST HATE TO BRING THIS UP

There are many other correlations, both with and without identifiable causes, having to do with what does and doesn't work in advertising. They have been scientifically tested and retested. I won't list them here because other authors have done so.[20]

Now, you may have noticed that something is conspicuously missing from this chapter's sampling of advertising correlations and causes. There is no mention of *great creative work* as a causal factor in marketing success. This isn't an oversight. Although many ad people claim to have found correlations between creativity in advertising and product sales, such claims are often flimsy, and in no case can causation be established. In many instances, the opposite has been shown: often what the industry hails as "great creative work" has no measurable effect on sales. Sometimes, in fact, so-called great creative work has been documented to drive sales *down*.

To automatically infer a causal correlation between award-winning and other forms of "great" advertising and sales is a potentially costly mistake.

I almost hate to bring it up. The hottest arguments about religion and politics pale in comparison to the squabbling of ad agencies over creativity: its role, its effects, its proper use, and which shops are truly creative versus those that merely think they are.

Shall we see if we can bring a voice of sanity to the topic? Critical thinking, I hope, will come to the rescue. Join me now for the Great Creativity Debate.

SUMMARY POINTS FROM
BEGUILED BY CORRELATION

- Our ability to detect correlations enhances our chance of survival, but it can also fool us.

(Continued)

- A single occurrence, no matter how remarkable or seemingly unlikely, is not a correlation.

- Many popular claims about correlations turn out not to be true.

- A correlation consists of two or more consistently co-inciding events.

- Finding a correlation doesn't mean you have found a cause.

- If the correlation is consistent, sometimes a marketer can make money without knowing the cause.

- But sometimes knowing the cause can save a market-er from loss and create opportunities for substantial gain.

5

THE GREAT CREATIVITY DEBATE

Direct marketers are often accused of having a bias against creativity.

At times I see why critics think so. Direct marketers love to talk about the importance of good targeting as the first priority, a strong offer as the second, and creative work as a distant third. Indeed, there is some evidence that if you get the first two right, you can shortchange the creative process and still generate a profit.

Which is regrettable. It's true that a good creative approach won't save a campaign from poor targeting or a weak offer, but it's also true that good creative work can dramatically increase sales once the targeting and offer are in place.

That's why smart direct marketers test creative approaches as well as targets and offers. You never know when changing *repair* to *fix* in your headline will increase sales 20 percent, as the legendary John Caples once found.[1]

But pendulums swing two ways. Just as some direct marketers are guilty of trivializing the importance of creative work, some advertisers are guilty of trying to enshrine Creativity as the Only Thing That Matters. In short, they will tell you that *if your advertising is truly creative, it will sell.*

This is patently false.

To debunk this silly notion, it may help to understand its origin. Just how did Creativity become King in some advertising agencies today?

ADVERTISING BEGINS

Advertising was inevitable from the moment humans learned to communicate. Even if most early words sounded like *aaarrrrggg*, pointing at a hungry lion and yelling *aaarrrrggg!* to warn your neighbors must certainly count as an advertisement.[2] Hardly the stuff of Clio Awards, but an advertisement nonetheless. A more advanced form of advertising known as the town crier couldn't have been far off.

Advertising advanced again when we invented writing. (Presumably, we invented reading at or about the same time.) Now it was possible to leave *aaarrrrggg* written in plain sight near the lion. No longer was it necessary to hang around to deliver the message in person. Not long after, merchants figured out they could enhance the town crier's effectiveness—or do away with the crier altogether—by hanging a poster in the window.

Two major inventions helped carry advertising from local to mass audiences. One was movable type. Printing had been around for a long time but for the most part had been used to print patterns on fabric, while reproducing documents remained in the hands of scribes. Movable type meant documents could be set up and printed faster than the fastest scribe ever dared dream. Mass printing was suddenly possible, and so, suddenly, was mass advertising.

The other invention that helped bring advertising to mass audiences was the railroad. Railroads made distribution to mass markets possible, and sellers of goods responded with mass production. Suddenly it was economically feasible to produce more goods than ever because you could ship and sell them throughout a large country.

Of course, your competitors could do so as well. This led to a need to: (1), find a way to persuade people to buy a product from a total, out-of-town stranger; and (2), find a way to ensure they bought your product instead of someone else's. The answer? Borrow an idea that open-range cattle ranchers had long employed to differentiate look-alike cattle: Mark your product with a proprietary brand. Soon, advertising began telling shoppers to look for specific brands instead of settling for imitations.

An early form of mass advertising arrived in the late 1800s with the invention of trade cards: calling cards with a marketing message on the back. At first, these were liberally handed out by *drummers* whose job was to drum up product sales. Later, trade cards showed up in stacks on countertops— the original point-of-sale advertising. Later still, they were attached to or inserted in product packaging. The cards themselves became collectibles, and their value as a medium and as a product in their own right shot up.

EARLY AD AGENCIES

Mass circulation publications arose alongside other mass products, and it wasn't long before merchants figured out that the pages of these publications were great places to sell their wares. They began purchasing small spaces in which to run announcements. This was the beginning of advertising as we know it today.

The increasing demand for space in publications led some enterprising people to visit major magazines and newspapers, buy pages from them in bulk at a negotiated discount, and resell them to marketers at full price. They called themselves advertising "agencies" because they acted as agents between buyers and sellers. Years would pass before it would cross their minds to provide creative services.

ADVERTISING GETS ITS BAD NAME

At first blush, it's tempting to say these early ads were not very creative. Copy was direct, and layouts were at best functional. But many of these early ads were extremely creative. Unfortunately, their creativity was often manifest in the audacity and outright dishonesty of their claims.

P. T. Barnum was one of America's earliest—and most successful—advertisers to give the profession a bad name. Posters screamed, "Look for it! Wait for it! See it!! It is Coming . . . P. T. Barnum's own and only GREATEST SHOW ON EARTH. . . . Vast in its proportions! High and pure in tone! Exalted in its aim! . . . The acme of refined elegance and best in all things." Puffery wasn't Barnum's only indulgence: He was given to blatant deception. People who paid to see a unicorn saw a rhinoceros instead. When a competitor paid handsomely for a rare, white Siamese elephant, Barnum stole his audience by painting one of his own elephants white.[3] An "inverted horse" turned out be a normal horse tethered by the tail. Spectators of limited vocabulary, expecting to see some sort of rare bird, eagerly went through a door marked "This way to the egress" only to find they had exited the building. They had to pay to re-enter.[4]

Patent medicine makers were quick to jump on the bandwagon and make outrageous claims of their own. Ads for Lydia Pinkham's Vegetable Compound, a patent medicine containing 20 percent alcohol, touted the compound as "A sure cure for PROLAPSUS UTERI, or falling of the womb and all FEMALE WEAKNESSES including leucorrhoea, irregular and painful menstruation, inflammation and ulceration of the womb, flooding, . . . for all weaknesses of the generative organs of either sex, it is second to no remedy that has ever been before the public, and for all diseases of the kidneys it is the GREATEST REMEDY IN THE WORLD."

Out-and-out scams using advertising to fleece the unwary spread. One advertisement in 1882 offered an authorized, color portrait of the late President James Garfield, ". . . approved by the President of the United States, by Congress and by every member of the President's family . . . executed by the Government's most expert steel engravers . . . from the original plate, in full colors approved by the Government . . . for one dollar each." For their dollar, customers received a five-cent postage stamp that featured Garfield's portrait. Another advertisement offered a surefire roach killer. What arrived in the mail were two blocks of wood with instructions to place the roach on one block and smash it with the other. Yet another offered a guaranteed method for making a good impression. For their money, hopefuls received instructions to sit on a pan of bread dough.

Those were the days of *caveat emptor*. Marketers could abuse trust with relative impunity because consumer protection laws didn't yet exist, and because buyers faced practical limitations pursuing companies that defrauded them from several states away.

So, despite honest advertisers—who did exist—advertising and mail-order scams flourished hand in hand. It wasn't long before both earned a bad name. Some 200 years later, we're still trying to shake it.[5]

CADILLAC DRIVES INTO THE GREAT DEBATE

In time, Congress passed laws, the U.S. Postal Service began cracking down on mail-order fraud, and advertising began cleaning up its act.

And significantly, ad agencies began offering "creative services" along with advertising space. Now you could hire an agency to write and lay out your ads, not just place them.

Still, ad writing tended to lean more toward the announcement side of things. When early ad man John E. Kennedy convinced Albert Lasker of the Lord & Taylor agency that advertising was no more or less than "salesmanship in print," the announcement approach began giving way to the hard-sell approach. Later, the nascent television advertising industry caught on and began recruiting carnival pitchmen to sell products on TV.[6] It worked.

But now and then, some renegade would create an ad that didn't announce and didn't sell hard. Probably the earliest and best known of these trend-buckers was an ad called "The Penalty of Leadership." Written for Cadillac Motors by Theodore MacManus, it ran once—just once—in the *Saturday Evening Post* on January 2, 1915.

What made the MacManus ad different was that it never mentioned Cadillac. In fact, it said nothing about cars at all. Rather, it presented a brilliantly written diatribe on the woes that leaders must endure. Were it not for the copyright notice, no one would have known it was an ad at all, much less for whom.

The ad was an instant hit. People from all over the United States wrote Cadillac for copies to display on their walls. The MacManus ad remains an advertising legend to this day. And it raised a serious question: Did advertising have to embody a rational sales pitch, as Kennedy advocated, or could advertising produce sales through indirect association and sheer literary craft, as the Theodore MacManus Cadillac ad seemed to have done?

Unfortunately, Cadillac *sales* were never linked to the ad. Its only measure of success was its own popularity. No matter, say some: the ad generated record awareness. Sales as a consequence were inevitable. Others respond that it's impossible to know how many cars Cadillac sold because of the ad, or how many cars Cadillac would have sold without it.

Thus begins the Great Creativity Debate.

THE CREATIVE REVOLUTION OF THE 1960s

Advertising continued on its way, sometimes with hard-sell ads, sometimes with more artistically executed soft-sell ads, sometimes with ads landing in between. Then, in the 1960s, Bill Bernbach came along.

His agency, Doyle Dane Bernbach, was famous for, among other efforts, its Volkswagen Beetle campaign. In an era when bigger was better, DDB dared to run an ad featuring a small photo of the car, surrounded by white space, over the headline, "Think small." A later ad broke all taboos with this single-word headline under a photo of the car: "Lemon."[7] Despite the taboos lying in tatters on the floor, Volkswagen Beetle sales took off.

DDB also rocked the advertising world when it created charmingly self-deprecating ads for its client Avis, not only admitting but touting its Number Two status in the car rental business. In its proposal stage, neither Bernbach nor Avis CEO Robert Townsend cared for the campaign, but Bernbach indicated that it was the best his agency had been able to come up with, and Townsend had earlier agreed to run whatever the agency recommended. Over the next two years, sales at Avis increased from 10 percent to 30 percent.

Something new was happening. Ads were *fun*. More ads that were fun followed. Benson & Hedges gave up talking about tobacco blends and taste to poke fun at the "disadvantages" of their longer cigarettes. Clairol dared to ask suggestively, "Does she . . . or doesn't she?" Sexy women emerged from Brylcreem Hair Groom tubes. A gorilla attacked bags checked at an airport to showcase the sturdiness of American Tourister luggage. Men dressed in naught but shirt, briefs, and socks hopped madly up and down to demonstrate that Burlington's over-the-calf socks stayed up.

Not only were ads suddenly becoming fun, but marketers daring to engage in fun advertising were seeing their sales soar.

Clearly, greater creative freedom in advertising was having a positive impact.

But it wasn't long before advertising pundits made an unwarranted leap. Many began to believe and preach that *creativity alone* was all it took to make products jump from shelves into shopping carts. The view persists today.

It is an error that needs debunking.

YOU CAN'T GET BACK THERE FROM HERE

Advertising's new focus on creativity for its own sake attracted a new breed to the field. What was once the domain of salespeople and business managers morphed into a golden opportunity for people with cool ideas. As creative advertising became the rule, the once-limited market for writers, designers, and filmmakers mushroomed. At last, artistes could use their creative talents to make a living outside of Hollywood, and without rich patrons or government grants.

But a funny thing happens when too many people imitate what began as unique: it ceases to be unique. When all advertising is "highly creative," none stands out. Thus, the stunning sales that rewarded early creative ads began to ebb. Those who still believed creativity was the sole source of advertising success defended their position using hindsight and selection bias: Creative campaigns that produced sales were successful because they were creative; and campaigns appearing to be creative that failed to produce sales must not have been "truly creative" after all.

People today are beleaguered by an ever-growing number of advertising messages conveyed by an ever-growing variety of media. In fact, it's not unusual for consumers to divide their attention among multiple media at the same time. A consumer can be and often is simultaneously involved in a TV show, a video game, a cell phone conversation, an MP3 player, and a magazine. Amid such clutter, some pundits blame any loss of advertising impact on a scarcity of true creativity. They mourn and advocate a return to the Creative Revolution of the 1960s. What we need, they'll tell you, is more Bill Bernbachs.

I have two news items for ad people who would return to the Creative Revolution of the 1960s:

1. *The Creative Revolution never left us.*   A continuing abundance of mundane advertising notwithstanding, all it takes is a look through publications like *Advertising Age, Adweek, Communication Arts, Creativity, US Ad Review,* and others to see that the spirit of "highly creative advertising" is alive, well, and thriving. The Creative Revolution was revolutionary in the 1960s because creativity for its own sake was largely unheard-of at that time. It no longer is. Today, ad agencies the world over champion creativity, publish books and articles about creativity, publicly lament when denied creative freedom, bestow awards for creativity, train viewers to expect creative commercials during the Super Bowl, and continually strive to out-create one another with their work. As a result, people are bombarded with more creative advertising today than they ever were in the 1960s. The net effect is that creativity in advertising is no longer revolutionary, no longer unique. Oxymoronically, the more creativity you have, the more commonplace creativity becomes. And when anything becomes commonplace, it ceases to stand out,[8] and its power necessarily wanes.

2. *It was the 1960s that left.*   The environment in which the Creative Revolution took the world by storm has changed. The Cold War, the Soviet Union, the Beatles, hippies, the Vietnam War, and protest songs are over. The Baby Boomers are seniors now. TV, radio, print, mail, and outdoor are no longer the only media. Wishing for creativity to work today as it did in the 1960s is like hoping that long hair on men will shock the older generation the way it did back then. We've moved on.

I realize this takes the wind out of reactionary sails. But hard as it may be to face, we're going to have to keep moving forward.

AGENCY WARS

A legacy left by the Creative Revolution is a prevailing advertising industry belief that True Creativity is the most important ingredient of successful advertising. Many ad agencies today measure True Creativity by the number of advertising industry awards a campaign wins.

Were it only that simple.

Not all ad agencies buy into the True Creativity legacy. Some do not view creativity as an advertising objective, nor do they view winning advertising awards as the prime indicator of an ad agency's ability. Well-crafted work is incontestably important, but is not the end in and of itself. Meeting objectives like making the cash register ring matter more.

Not that we ad agencies who eschew the True Creativity legacy eschew creativity itself. On the contrary, we embrace it as a vital ingredient in advertising success. But we do not believe that advertising success results from creativity alone. To say that good creativity in advertising inevitably leads to sales is like saying that dressing impeccably for an interview ensures you'll get the job. It would be tantamount to mistaking an ingredient for the formula.

The Great Creativity Debate leads to admittedly petty bickering between the two kinds of agencies. The debate often goes something like this:

Results Proponents: You are artistes who don't know how to sell.

Creative Proponents: Your stuff is by the rules, uninspired, and often embarrassing to boot.

Results Proponents: You waste money fulfilling your own artistic yearnings at the client's expense.

Creative Proponents: Originality is needed to break through and get noticed, and quality reflects on the brand.

Results Proponents: Breaking through and getting noticed doesn't mean you sold a thing.

Creative Proponents: Don't get noticed and you won't sell a thing.

Results Proponents: If it doesn't sell, it's not creative.

Creative Proponents: If it's not creative, it won't sell.

Results Proponents: Your work is irresponsible.

Creative Proponents: You are the antichrists of creativity.

In hopes of rising above the bickering (and at some risk of escalating it instead), I am going to present the main points of the True Creativity position. I shall do my best to represent them in fairness. This is important because I next intend to debunk them, and I really don't care to waste time debunking what no one ever said.

THE *TRUE CREATIVITY* POSITION

Advertising people who believe that creativity is the best measure of good advertising tend to proffer the following arguments:

- There is a correlation between award-winning advertising and successful products.

- There is a correlation between likable advertising and successful products.

- There is a correlation between advertising with high recall scores and successful products.

- There is a correlation between noncreative advertising and unsuccessful products.

- The above-mentioned correlations are too strong to be coincidence.

- Numerous studies have correlated creative advertising with sales success.

- Advertising history brims with an abundance of cases in which highly creative, disruptive, fresh, award-caliber advertising has helped bring a product to market dominance.

- Many successful ad campaigns said little or nothing about the product for sale. Sheer creativity made the difference.

- Advertising creates the only opportunity for parity products like beer, wireless networks, and banks to compete. When these use truly creative advertising, they win market share. This is evidence of the power of creative advertising.

- Creativity is a tool for making advertising stand out. Failure to be creative can mean fading into the background where no one notices your ad at all.

- "Advertising is fundamentally persuasion, and persuasion happens to be an art, not a science."—Bill Bernbach

You may believe that each of these points represents a sound argument. But if you read Chapter 3, you know not to mistake a sound argument for proof.

That said, let's apply a little critical thinking.[9]

LET'S BEGIN WITH THOSE CORRELATIONS

There's no reason we can't lump the first five arguments together, and dispatch them together as well, since, as you'll note, they all rely on correlation:

- There is a correlation between award-winning advertising and successful products.

- There is a correlation between likable advertising and successful products.
- There is a correlation between advertising with high recall scores and successful products.
- There is a correlation between noncreative advertising and unsuccessful products.
- The above-mentioned correlations are too strong to be coincidence.

If you're truly committed to finding correlations between award-winning advertising, likable advertising, highly recalled advertising, and successful products, chances are you will. What remains to be seen is whether you'll be able to find *causation*.

What would it take to establish causation? I'm afraid an appeal to common sense won't do. Statistical integrity demands that we concede at least a modicum of common sense among at least some of the people who took Orson Welles's radio broadcast of *War of the Worlds* for a real attack, believed Procter & Gamble's logo was a demonic symbol, found O. J. Simpson not guilty, or expected to find weapons of mass destruction in Iraq.

If you want to determine whether creativity is the cause behind the correlations, you must eliminate all other possible causes. Other possible causes might include an economic shift, weather changes, tariffs, a celebrity mention, terrorist activity, happenstance, reaching what Malcolm Gladwell calls a tipping point, a declaration of war—the list goes on. To complicate matters, no two successful products need necessarily have attained their success because of the same cause. We may be looking for a new cause in each new case.

Eliminating alternate causes isn't easily done, if for no other reason than that all contingencies are not easily identified, especially after the fact. Who knows what we might overlook? Maybe the packaging color came suddenly into vogue. Maybe a group of environmentalists found your product to be earth-friendly or called for a boycott of your competitor's product. Maybe a leading transcendentalist found it calming. Coca-Cola sales are brisk in San Juan de Chamula, Mexico, not because of advertising, but because a Catholic congregation there embraced a local folkloric belief that burping rids them of evil spirits. Who knows what effect undetected factors such as these might have on sales? If you don't know it's there, how do you rule it out?

And let's not overlook the possibility that we might have the causation backward. Perhaps the very fact of a product's popularity allows a marketer to engage in more creative advertising. As previously mentioned, *Freakonomics* authors Steven D. Levitt and Stephen J. Dubner build a compelling case along that line in regards to marketing political candidates. They found that candidates *already likely to win* were more successful at raising funds and thus were able to spend more on advertising. Although it might appear at first blush that more spending on advertising helps candidates win, upon closer inspection, we come to find that the reverse may be true: winning allows for more ad spending. In like manner, there may be instances where success at the cash register came first and enabled creative advertising later. Even Budweiser's entertaining spots— from talking lizards to fire-breathing dinner dates—came well after the brand established itself as a leader.

For the sake of argument, let's assume that we have identified all alternate explanations for a product's success. To prove creativity-as-cause, we must now set up controlled experiments to eliminate all other possible causes until creativity survives as the only possible remaining cause. (It goes without saying that creativity must be subjected to and survive the same experiments.) This means we'll need groups that are exposed to the advertising and the other factors, groups that are exposed to the advertising without the other factors, groups that are exposed to the other factors without the advertising, and groups that are exposed to neither. All other conditions among the groups must be identical.

It gets harder. Factors responsible for one product's success may be irrelevant to another's, so these tests must be conducted product by product, case by case. We'll have to test a large sample and array of products—not just a handful—before we can say with near certainty[10] that it was the creativity, the likability, or the staying power of an ad that made a product succeed.

Here's another problem. What exactly *is* creativity? How do you pinpoint what is creative in an ad, and separate it from the rest of the ad? Was the headline creative? The copy? The layout? The photo? The look on the model's face? The font? The white space? The way all these elements interact? How do you isolate and test these elements? How do you separate *true* creativity from creativity in the eye of the beholder? One of my earliest successful ads was a painfully straightforward execution that proved immensely profitable at the cash register. Did I say, "painfully straightforward"? A colleague praised the ad as "very creative in its use of straightforwardness."

Finally, for a perfectly valid test of an already completed campaign, we would have to re-create the economic, cultural, and other circumstances that existed when the campaign originally ran. Which, of course, isn't possible.

What *is* possible, however, is to plan and build such testing into the next campaign *in advance*.[11, 12] Proponents of True Creativity generally do not do this. Too often their evaluations, when conducted, take place post-campaign and rely on the likes of correlation, *post hoc, ergo propter hoc*, moving goalposts, hindsight bias, and other shaky methods. I don't accuse them of deliberately suppressing information or avoiding feedback; it's more of an unwitting oversight. Most advertising agencies simply aren't trained in measurable techniques, much less critical thinking. They have been groomed by an industry that makes the unfounded claim that rationalism needlessly fetters creativity. Moreover, clients tend not to demand measurable advertising from their agencies, but instead push for campaigns that they *like*. Until this situation changes, agencies will remain free to cook up their wildest ideas on naught but the *assumption* that such generate sales.

CREATIVITY THAT FAILS AT THE CASH REGISTER

If we could find highly creative ad campaigns that failed to produce sales, we might at least cast doubt upon creativity as the *sole* required ingredient to advertising success.

Alka Seltzer's "I can't believe I ate the whole thing" campaign was immensely popular, was highly praised for its creativity, and is still fondly recalled 40 years after its passing. Alka Seltzer sales went down during the campaign.

The New Coke campaign won awards, enjoyed great popularity (spokes-character Max Headroom even landed his own TV show), and is still easily recalled. But you may have noticed a scarcity of New Coke on the shelves at your local grocer.

The "milk mustache" campaign wins awards, is immensely popular (stars readily agree to pose), and enjoys widespread awareness and recall. Yet milk sales haven't budged. (Some might rebut that the campaign was successful because, *without* it, milk sales might have *declined*. This is a weak argument, for three reasons: (1) Without a control group, there's no way to establish what would have happened to milk sales without the campaign; (2) If the objective is to increase sales, then maintaining sales isn't, by definition, a success; (3) If sales remained level after a large advertising expense, the cost per item sold went *up*. From that standpoint, one could argue that the mustache campaign was not helpful, but harmful.)

More recently, the Miller Brewing Company abandoned its highly creative, immensely popular "Man Law" campaign. It seems that the brewer's beer sales plummeted, even as the campaign established a firm foothold in American pop culture. Even Aflac announced plans to challenge its ubiquitous quacking duck campaign in favor of tactics that sell harder. Opinion remains divided on whether the recently-retired Wendy's campaign, in which a non-herd-follower sporting red pigtails, was truly creative or truly annoying. In any case, sales dropped during the campaign.

Do the exceptions prove anything? Only that highly creative advertising doesn't *ensure* market success. That alone should tell you something. A hot, creative concept doesn't necessarily mean you're on the road to cash registers ringing out of control.

THE UNLIKELY COINCIDENCE

A number of successful products have highly creative advertising. As the cases pile up, someone inevitably decides that the correlation is too strong for all but the most stubborn to dismiss as coincidence.

Here's the problem with such thinking. If highly creative advertising linked to highly successful products proves creativity is the prime success factor, what do ad campaigns that *aren't* highly creative but are still linked to highly successful products prove? Such cases abound: Westinghouse, The Sharper Image, Windex, Nordstrom, Alpo, The Home Depot, Lowe's, and Macy's, to name a few. If successful, noncreative campaigns can be disqualified as coincidence, so can successful, creative campaigns. You can't have it both ways.

With any fortuitous alignment of events, it's tempting—and human—to dismiss coincidence. Take, for instance, lottery winners. Most have a back story ("I almost didn't buy a ticket, but something told me to try"), an urgent financial need ("I was behind on my rent"), and an experience with a last-minute, funny feeling ("I had a feeling as they were about to announce the winner"). It's all too much, they assure themselves, for mere coincidence to explain. The stars and planets (or their equivalent) must have aligned in their favor.

Meanwhile, vast numbers of people with similar feelings, experiences, and financial needs *didn't* win. If wins defy coincidence, so must losses. This would have to mean that the stars and planets equally aligned to the detriment of the millions of entrants who walked away empty-handed.

The lesson here is that it's easy to be overwhelmed by big anecdotes with big numbers. Don't be.

THE BURDEN OF DISPROOF

On February 15, 2001, the Fox network aired a pseudo-exposé called *Conspiracy Theory: Did We Land on the Moon?*

In just one hour, Fox irresponsibly convinced millions of Americans that the 1969 lunar landing was a hoax. Thanks to the program, some 40 years after the lunar landing actually happened, scientists still have their hands full debunking the show—not to mention numerous and equally erroneous books, articles, and videos.

Such myth building takes naught but a quick, ill-informed statement and a willingly gullible audience. Cleaning up the mess and setting the record straight by those who know what they're talking about can involve a mountain of work that takes years.

It happens in marketing too. One brief story about marketers rocketing to success on the heels of a highly creative campaign can convince generations of advertisers that Creativity is King. Digging out facts and setting things straight takes time, research, brains, and hard work. In science, someone gets around to that kind of debunking sooner or later. In marketing, hardly anyone bothers, so the myths stand uncontested, and more myths are built upon them.

CASE STUDY: HARLEY-DAVIDSON

When it comes to marketing misinformation that tends to endure unhampered by reason, the relatively recent resurgence of Harley-Davidson sales presents a good case study. Harley's recovery has been heralded as proof of the power of creative advertising, because at first glance no other factor appears to account for the company's turnaround. But diligent homework reveals much to challenge this particular god of the gaps. By the early 1980s, Harley sales were falling fast. Sales picked up—dramatically—and stayed up at about the same time that a respected advertising agency launched a highly creative campaign for the legendary

bike. From the perspective of creativity-solves-all proponents, this case proves the power of creativity.

Until, that is, you take a second glance and look at other
factors.

In 1982, President Reagan raised the tariff on Japanese
motorcycle imports, and not just a little. He took it from
4.4 percent to 49.4 percent. It would be naïve to believe
that advertising brought about Harley's resurgence with
no help from government's leveling of the price playing
field between Japanese imports and American brands like
Harley.

At the same time, a wave of "buy American" sentiment
washed across the nation. Harley rode the wave. Quite
apart from its advertising, Harley played on American
sympathies and positioned itself as a valuable piece of
America's heritage, an underdog worthy of preservation.

Meanwhile, motorcycle groups espousing worthy causes
began popping up, one of the most notable being Bikers
Against Child Abuse (BACA). Even the Hell's Angels
themselves began to combat their lawless image by becoming a bona fide not-for-profit organization.

Also about that time, Baby Boomers, who had witnessed
the hippie movement from their teen and young adult
years, entered the ranks of people with sufficient dispos-
able income to purchase and ride a Hog. Hogs had always
been cool to this more open-minded demographic. Now
well into their careers, they could afford them.

Looking back, who's to say that highly creative advertising accounted for Harley's turnaround? Maybe it was
Reagan. Maybe it was BACA. Maybe it was patriotism. Or
Boomers. Or a combination of all of these. Or some other
factor that escaped notice. Years after the fact, there's no
way to know.

"NUMEROUS STUDIES HAVE
CORRELATED . . ."

The next argument for True Creativity also appeals to correlations as proof: "Numerous studies have correlated creative advertising with sales success."

But unlike the earlier arguments, this one cites an alleged convergence of "numerous studies." This is less easily dismissed by a mere reiteration of the fact that correlation doesn't guarantee causation, so let's look at the studies themselves. Granted the possibility of definitive studies that I have missed, of the many I have reviewed, I offer the following observations:

1. *The studies fail to agree on a useful definition of creativity.* Some studies focus on a campaign's likability. Others focus on the use of humor. Some look at emotional appeal, drama, editing and pacing, audacity of the concept, finessing of an execution, or sometimes even a poor, inept execution (because it "stands out," making it paradoxically creative in its own right). Some studies embrace more than one of these definitions at once. This is a problem because a broad definition of creativity allows virtually any campaign to qualify as *creative*, and, for that matter, any campaign not to.[13] If that is true, then we must conclude that it is *advertising itself* that correlates with sales, not creativity. But this rather negates the whole creativity argument.

To narrow things back down, we should evaluate the *quality* of the creative work. Fine, but now we're back where we started. How does one distinguish *quality* creative work from *ordinary* creative work? Some would argue that the Haggar "making things right" commercials are creative, while others might call them offensive for would-be comedic use of bullying and intolerance to sell clothing. Some find Burger King's commercials with a speechless, BK mask-wearing loiterer creative, while others find them creepy. These are wholly subjective determinations that inevitably lead to circular reasoning like this: "A campaign that we *knew* was creative drove sales up. This proves the power of creativity. A campaign that we *thought* was creative turned out not to be because sales went down. This proves that noncreative advertising doesn't sell."

2. *The studies fail to control for outside factors.* If you raise two plants from cloned seeds, but in different soil and weather conditions, one plant will grow taller and healthier than the other. The healthy development of a plant hinges on more than the quality of the seed alone. In short, there are other factors.

Advertising doesn't exist in a vacuum, either. Many outside factors can affect marketing outcomes. Budgets can have much to do with a campaign's success. Poorly funded campaigns reach fewer people less often, so they must work harder to compete against well-funded campaigns. Media choices matter, too. A message that performs well in one medium may be less effective in another. When government forced cigarette advertising from the airwaves to the printed page, the Marlboro cowboy lost the use of its legendary soundtrack taken from the movie *The Magnificent Seven* and, with it, lost considerable impact.

The news, political, and cultural environment can also affect results. A news item in *Life* magazine that listed the Ian Fleming novel *From Russia With Love* as one of President John Kennedy's favorites boosted sales of the book and led to its being chosen as the basis for the second James Bond film. The political climate at the outset of the war in Iraq negatively affected sales of products associated with France. A cultural shift toward better health and nutrition forced Post cereals to change its popular spokes-toon's name from Sugar Bear to Super Bear.

A study that ignores outside factors risks hastiness in crediting—or blaming—creativity for results. Creativity can reign as a sole determiner only when all other factors are isolated and controlled. A historical look that links creative campaigns with successful products doesn't come close to doing that.

3. *Many studies, no matter how scholarly in their approach, remain anecdotal.* Stories are not proof (as noted in Chapter 3). Only when the vast majority of creative campaigns can be *demonstrated*—not just alleged—to outperform can we draw a correlation.[14] Even then, causation is another matter (for reasons explained in Chapter 4).

4. *Many of these studies are conducted by people actively seeking the very conclusions they find.* Let's be honest here. Advertising agencies *want* creativity to be proven effective. It's a big part of what they sell. So do clients who bet big bucks on highly creative work. When these people research the effectiveness of creativity, bias is inevitable.

Do not bother with indignant protests of integrity and good intentions. The most seasoned professionals and academicians with the best intentions fall prey, which is why double-blind controls have become a scientific standard. If you set out with an interest in corroborating what you are inclined to believe, you will find exactly what you're looking for, no matter how unbiased you think you are.

If you don't believe me, here's an experiment you can try. Ask a sample of people to evaluate a resumé. Ahead of time, tell half of them that the applicant is of higher socio-economic status. Tell the other half that the applicant is of lower socioeconomic status. Chances are you'll find that the first group looks upon the applicant more favorably than the second.

I am open to any valid study that proves that creativity is the one key. As yet, I haven't found one.

MORE ABOUT ANECDOTES

Sooner or later, every myth-buster deals with, "Oh yeah? How do you explain the time that . . ." Advertising lore is replete with such rebuttals. An abundance of stories appear, at first glance, to leave no room for any conclusion other than "creativity made the difference." Such classic God-in-the-Gaps reasoning is summed up nicely in these two arguments:

- Advertising history brims with cases in which highly creative, disruptive, fresh, award-caliber advertising has helped bring a product to market dominance.

- Many successful ad campaigns said little or nothing about the product for sale. Sheer creativity made the difference.

It's true that advertising history brims with cases in which highly creative, disruptive, fresh, award-caliber advertising has helped bring a product to market dominance. It's also true that many successful ad campaigns said little or nothing about the product for sale.

Both arguments can be put quickly to rest. They are based on anecdotes, and again, anecdotes may be suggestive but are never proof. If you know a number of people who were bitten by German Shepherds and no one who was bitten by another breed, you don't know that German Shepherds bite more than other breeds.[15]

Short of controlled testing, there is no basis for concluding that sheer creativity made the difference.

I should add that advertising history also brims with an abundance of cases in which perfectly straightforward advertising paid out big. For proof, search your kitchen, bathroom, and garage for name-brand products whose advertising is mundane or even nonexistent.

There are also numerous cases of so-called creative advertising, that received wide recognition yet failed to produce. Consider MasterCard's "Priceless" campaign. Or, consider how Taco Bell sales plunged while their spokes-Chihuahua's popularity rose, yet rebounded when the chain retired the creative pooch in favor of the more straightforward, traditional elements of sizzling ingredients and price deals.

ABOUT THOSE PARITY PRODUCTS

- Advertising creates the only opportunity for parity products like beer, wireless networks, and banks to compete. When these use truly creative advertising, they win market share. This is evidence of the power of creative advertising.

Respected voices echo the sentiment. On the front page of its April 7, 2008, issue, no less than *Advertising Age* claimed, "Bud Light got to No. 1 by providing three decades of nearly uninterrupted chucklehead, frat-boy humor." This genre of assertion is so embedded in advertising lore that it's not unusual for marketers to nod their heads in unthinking agreement. But asserting isn't proving. It is true that Bud Light has served up 30 years of frat-boy humor. It is true that Bud Light leads the pack. But to infer that the first brought about the second requires making a few leaps, including *post hoc, ergo propter hoc*, mistaking an argument for proof, and confirmation bias, to name a few. Invoking *Advertising Age* doesn't help. It only serves to add the logical fallacy "Argument from Authority" to the list of leaps.

I would be the last to disagree that a strong brand is vital for helping out a parity product. But a strong brand and highly creative advertising needn't and often do not come in pairs. A strong brand results from a combination of factors. Highly creative advertising may or may not be one of them. As of this writing, Starbucks, Barnes & Noble, and Nordstrom all fit neatly into parity categories and do very little advertising. What little they do would not be characterized as highly creative. Yet each has a strong brand.

Creative advertising can be a powerful tool but is at best an expression of the brand—not the brand itself.[16]

ABOUT THE NEED TO STAND OUT

- Creativity is a tool for making advertising stand out. Failure to be creative can mean fading into the background where no one notices your ad at all.

It doesn't take a lot of experimentation to confirm that advertising that fails to draw notice also fails to produce sales.

But to assume that highly creative work is the *only* way that work draws notice is a leap. No one would dispute the success of home shopping channels. While their approach is arguably creative from a direct marketing standpoint, it would be a stretch to call them *creative* in the traditional advertising sense.

Creativity is but one tool (which breaks into multiple tools itself). Another tool is relevance. Another is the clear promise of a strong benefit. Another is a compelling incentive offer. Another is timing. Another is targeting. The list goes on.

Sometimes mundane, practical solutions outshine so-called highly creative ones. When the American Institute of Banking wanted to draw more attention from branch managers to a particular ad, I suggested putting "BANK MANAGERS," just like that, in all caps, at the top of the ad. When an unknown burger store wasn't pulling in diners, I noted there was no picture or mention of a burger in their signage and suggested they add one. When a retail client's customers complained of trouble finding the parking lot entrance, I suggested directional signs. In each not-so-creative case, sales went immediately up.[17]

Another leap comes in the form of assuming that drawing notice is, in and of itself, successful advertising. This is simply not true. The Ford Edsel drew notice. So did New Coke. So did Miller's Man Law. So did the class clown and the class nerd in my high school. But Edsel, New Coke, and Miller's Man Law didn't sell, and the class clown and the class nerd didn't get dates. Attention does not equal success.

ON ADVERTISING AS ART

- "Advertising is fundamentally persuasion, and persuasion happens to be an art, not a science."—Bill Bernbach

Like most people with a passion for marketing history, I am a Bill Bernbach fan, and I have great regard for his impact on the advertising industry. Yet even the most ardent follower must concede that a Bernbach quote isn't de facto viable, and certainly isn't canon. (Yes, it's "Argument from Authority" again.) That said, let's go ahead and deal with what is possibly the advertising world's most oft-quoted Bernbachism on its own terms.

My friend Danny once chastised me for alleging that being an auto mechanic was more of a science than an art. His father was a mechanic. Danny said, "He could diagnose your car's problem just by placing his hand flat on the hood while the motor was running. If that's not an art, what is?"

So perhaps there's a bit of art and science to everything we do.[18]

Bill Bernbach died in 1982, but ad people the world over still revere and quote him. Rightly so. And his point is well taken: without a doubt, persuasion—selling—is an art. But like it or not, the fact remains that there is a science to diagnosing car troubles, and there is also a science to selling.

The science of selling is a difficult one to measure—how do you quantify handshakes, smiles, small talk, timing, and more?—but we're making headway. Studies described in books like Paco Underhill's *Why We Buy: The Science of Shopping*, Neil Rackham's *Spin Selling*, and even the now-corny but still insightful *Tested Advertising Methods* by John Caples provide great starting points.

If you must cling to the notion that selling is an art *only*, please note that Bernbach never said that advertising is an art *form*. Advertising wasn't invented to be framed, hung on a wall, and admired—even though it's admittedly gratifying when that happens. It is manifest only when advertising hits its target in accordance with agreed-upon objectives.

Which is why Bernbach also said, "Technique for its own sake can be dangerous. . . . You're so anxious to do things differently . . . and more brilliantly than the next guy, that that becomes the goal of the ad, instead of selling the merchandise."[19]

Results and acclaim needn't be mutually exclusive, but to assume that one ensures the other is frivolous, irresponsible, and naïve.

Many successful salespeople make lousy entertainers. Many top-selling ads make lousy art. But when it comes to the art of persuasion, only those that sell are the masters.

IN DEFENSE OF CREATIVITY

At the outset of this chapter, I said there is evidence that good targeting and a strong offer can generate a profit, even if the advertising itself is uncreative. This has been repeatedly borne out by numerous, highly profitable direct response campaigns that earn a big fat zero on any creativity scale. Flip through any in-flight magazine or other publication carrying full-page mail order ads. Those ugly layouts comprising nothing but dense type, a blustering headline, and a corny coupon? Marketers don't persist in running such ads month after month because they are ineffective. Such ads are big money-generators.[20]

For an even less-creative example, consider the credit card offers you receive almost daily from Citi, Chase, and Capital One. All say pretty much the same thing in pretty much the same way, and consistently pull responses in the range of 0.4 to 0.6 percent—enough to earn a profit. Because credit card direct marketers know that most of their success comes from sending a low introductory rate offer to the right people at the right time, many give only token attention to crafting a compelling message. Those who do so risk missing an opportunity to sell even more. Over a century of testing and experience shows that although good targeting and a sound offer with weak creative work can in some instances generate sales, strengthening the creative work can take that success to the next level.

In my own agency we have proven this claim a number of times. For a major credit card issuer, we traded the standard approach for a warm, personal one—and beat the average industry response five-to-one. To rule out flukes, we remailed twice and attained the same results. We had the same mailing list other banks use and, frankly, a weaker incentive rate offer. Working with the creative approach alone increased sales.

When a bank asked us to beat their full-page ad running in the Bay Area, we replaced the headline and copy while leaving the offer and media schedule intact. Account openings directly attributable to the ad doubled. Then we went to work on their radio spot, again leaving the schedule and offer intact. Account openings attributable directly to *that* increased *sevenfold*.

In yet another instance, a client's sales *doubled* as the result of a good rewrite.

A subscription offer created by *Kiplinger's Personal Finance* magazine also illustrates. When they changed the colors of the mailing envelope and added the words, "Do not bend," subscription sales went up. Numerous other direct marketers have found that, once the market and offer are squared away, testing changes in the creative approach can be profitable.[21]

Still, it's important to realize there are limits to what creativity can do. Creativity cannot rescue a product no one wants. And it cannot overcome impediments like a weak strategy, poor targeting, a non-compelling offer, or the absence of an offer.

Everything in its place.

ARTISTIC MARKETING

Sometimes I think it's unfortunate that the advertising industry shares the same media used by the entertainment industry. It confuses us. It makes it easy to sit back and admire our work for its own sake, rather than as a selling tool. Or, it lulls us into thinking that aesthetics and popularity are one and the same with effectiveness.

Marketing *should* be artistic. Its approach, design, and tone reflect upon the marketer. And good, creative executions can take successful targeting and offers and make them even more successful.

But the moment artistry becomes the sole objective, agencies should quit charging fees and apply for grants instead.

SUMMARY POINTS FROM *THE GREAT CREATIVITY DEBATE*

- Creativity in advertising can make a huge difference in sales.

- Creativity should neither be dismissed as irrelevant, nor enshrined as all that matters.

- Early "creativity" often consisted of spurious claims. It didn't help the profession's image.

- A 1915 ad for Cadillac introduced an indirect, creative approach that sent advertising in a new direction.

- Many people still believe the aptly named *Creative Revolution* of the 1960s permanently enthroned creativity as the determining force behind successful advertising. A closer look reveals that the real determining force may have been the newness of the Creative Revolution itself, which wore off, and the environment in which it flourished, which has since changed.

(Continued)

- Correlations between highly successful products and highly creative advertising prove nothing (see Chapter 4).
- No causal relationship between *creativity alone* and sales has been demonstrated.
- Studies fail to prove that creativity as generally defined by the advertising industry is a sure bet for increasing sales.
- Creativity is one of many important tools advertisers wield.
- When good targeting and a compelling offer are already in place, creativity, here defined as "a clear, hard-to-ignore, believable, accessible, compelling, selling message," has been shown to be a powerful force for increasing sales.
- Though advertising and entertainment share the same media, do not mistake entertainment and artistry for advertising that sells.

6

A CRITICAL LOOK AT BRANDING

This is embarrassing.

As champions of instant, measurable results, direct response people are supposed to dismiss any form of advertising that doesn't make the phone ring and ring now.

Yet here I am, confessing a passion for—of all things—branding.

Branding, as you might imagine, is not typically what direct response agencies, like the one where I work, do. Except, well, yes it is. Because all advertising, including direct response, affects the brand.

Every commercial for Time-Life Books builds a brand. So does every J. Peterman, Levenger, and Sharper Image catalog. So does every ACLU, AARP, and AAA direct mailing. So does every page on Amazon.com. And so does every Ron Popeil infomercial.

Even a message, whose sole objective is to produce orders, leaves an impression about the advertiser. Responsible direct marketers understand the importance of leaving the *right* impression and of leaving it on purpose. They recognize that direct response advertising influences all within its reach, not just the relatively few who actually respond. A chance to leave a strong impression with the *nonresponding* majority is a bonus marketing opportunity only a fool would waste. Moreover, smart direct marketers build their strategies upon the brand.

I suspect it isn't branding itself that direct marketers disdain so much as the abundant abuses that *pass* for branding. On this point, despite any other differences, responsible direct response marketers find themselves in full agreement with responsible branding agencies.

WHAT BRANDING ISN'T

Occasionally I stumble upon a company that proudly tells me they have just, at no small cost, revitalized and redefined their brand. Then they lay a slogan on me—usually a lame one with the word *people* in it[1]—and show me a new or updated logo. They are so pleased with themselves and the fruits of their investment that, in an uncharacteristic show of restraint, I keep my mouth shut. This is not the time to tell them that a slogan and a logo do not a brand make.

There are as many definitions of branding as there are branding agencies and consultants. I define a brand as *the sum total of your values, as evidenced by how you deliver on those values, at every point of contact.*

Your brand is what you stand for and what you *won't* stand for. It is your company's personality. It is how you will and won't do business. It is the customers you seek and the ones you don't. It is how you treat employees, part-ners, vendors, and customers. It is the care that goes into your product or service. It is your overriding principles and your diligence in adhering to them.

To the extent that you ride herd on your brand, it is man-ifest in the look and feel of your facilities, in the behavior of your employees, and in all of your communications—in person, in policy, on the phone, online, in correspondence, and in advertising.

In short, a brand is the values that you, your company, and your people *live*.

Advertising does not create a brand. In fact, some of to-day's strongest brands belong to remarkably quiet adver-tisers. There is no Nordstrom campaign touting impeccable service and upscale decor, no Barnes & Noble campaign ex-tolling a book lover's hangout with enthusiasts eager to help you find obscure titles, no Starbucks campaign brag-ging about the aficionado behind the counter who can tell you the differences between coffees from around the world.

These companies have built strong brands through con-sistent *delivery*, which is the outgrowth of *values* backed by *passion*.

And they all managed to do it without help from slogans like, "Nordstrom. Great service, real marble floors."[2,3]

A BIT OF BRANDING HISTORY

Originally, *branding* referred to burning one's mark on bo-vine hips to help ranchers distinguish among look-alike cattle.

We have the advent of the railroad to thank for the term's induction into the marketing lexicon. Railroads made mass distribution possible, which, in turn, made mass production viable. With them came knockoffs, and with knockoffs came the need for manufacturers to differentiate their products. They solved the problem by adding proprietary marks to their packaging, and began referring to the practice with the aptly appropriated term *branding*.

Branding worked. Consumers began lining up behind preferred brands, and it wasn't long before brands became valuable assets in and of themselves. Companies protected their brands by standardizing trademark use, prosecuting unauthorized use of names and trademarks, and—if they were smart—refusing to put their marks on products that didn't live up to their standards.

Brand preference evolved in two directions. The first centers around *product attributes*: Ruffles have ridges, Heinz ketchup is thickest. The second centers around creating a *product image* to appeal to the self-concept of the market: a Levi's wearer would rather die than wear Wranglers. And vice versa.

Image marketing proved a useful solution for products with little else to distinguish them—at first. Suddenly, a brand could wishfully think up an image for itself and attract customers who identified with it. After an unsuccessful foray as a woman's cigarette, Marlboro reintroduced itself as the cigarette for manly men. Powerful TV spots featured ruggedly handsome cowboys, puffing away as they herded cattle to music from *The Magnificent Seven*. Soon any male smoker who wanted to look manly *had* to be seen smoking Marlboro, and would pay for the privilege.

Other brands without a readily apparent competitive advantage were quick to differentiate by image as well. Substance became optional. For a while and in quite a few cases, it worked. Pepsi became the cola for young people expressing individuality. Ultra Brite became the toothpaste for people with sex appeal. Jif became the peanut butter for choosy mothers.

But as brands and choices proliferated and as consumers paid more attention to benefit for price paid, brand loyalty began eroding. All but the fussiest consumers began figuring out that choosing Hunt's, Heinz, or Del Monte tomato sauce had little effect on the outcome of their lasagna. They learned that briefs from J. C. Penney performed about the same as briefs from Fruit of the Loom. They noticed their cars handled equally well with radials from Goodyear or Sears.[4]

The unthinkable was happening: Despite distinctive trademarks and carefully crafted images, well-known brands were becoming parity products. Even the cowboy lost his hold,[5] and mighty Marlboro found itself committing the ultimate brand no-no: *lowering price to compete.*

PSEUDO BRANDING

Justifiably panicked, marketers today have reacted by becoming increasingly evangelical about the need to build and maintain powerful brands. That's a good idea. It becomes a bad idea when they think they can still build a strong brand with advertising alone.

Times have changed. Linking your brand to a cowboy is no longer enough. After 50 years of shallow images and incessant clutter, consumers are no longer so easily charmed. Today, the practice of claiming to be unique without bothering to change anything but your advertising is *pseudo branding.*

More and more companies, stuck in the past, fall prey to pseudo branding. A company runs a campaign telling you they really are different in the way they think, hire, and behave. But upon visiting their place of business, you find a bank, a grocery store, an insurance company, or a department store that looks, feels, and acts like any other. This is not branding. It is letting your customer down.

Some companies come up with a slogan that means a good deal to the board of directors and their relatives, but to no one else. At a recent convention, I came upon yet another exhibitor using the headline, "We Care." I asked the marketing team how they felt about the line. Their answer was revealing: "We know that everyone says 'We care.' But the other guys just *say* it. We *really mean it*, and we think our customers can tell." This is not branding. It is talking to yourself.[6]

Today's consumers demand more than pretension or declarations of quality. They demand substance. At the cash register, they reward those who deliver it to them.

TEST YOURSELF: HOW STRONG IS YOUR BRAND?

Do you have a strong brand? Here are some revealing, proprietary questions we put our own clients through as we work to understand who they are, and who their customers are.

Caution: Denial is seductive. It's easier to tell yourself you have a strong brand than it is to take an honest look. Even the most seasoned executives are good at kidding themselves when it comes to questions like these:[7]

1. The *Masked Logo* Test—If you covered up your logo, would customers be able to tell you from the competition by the experience you, your product, or your service creates? Could customers tell they were in your facility by the feel, the decor, and the way they were treated? A yes indicates a strong brand. A no indicates you have work to do.

2. The *Fickle Customer* Test—Would your customers readily jilt you for a lower-priced look-alike? A no indicates a strong brand. A yes indicates you have work to do.

3. The *Oh, Come On* Test—Do people believe your claims or pass them off as empty corporate boasting? A yes indicates a strong brand. A no indicates you have work to do.

4. The *Value Statement Transplant* Test—If you wrote and framed a summary of your values as you see them, could competitors get away with hanging the same document in their own halls? A no indicates a strong brand. A yes indicates you have work to do.

5. The *Do Your Employees Get It?* Test—Do your employees know, get behind, and help deliver what you stand for? For that matter, do *you?* Are your employees on the bandwagon? Do they even know where the bandwagon is? Don't let yourself off easy by reassuring yourself that your employees read the mission statement and can recite your slogan. The question is whether *your values* have become part of *their behavior* on the job. A yes indicates a strong brand. A no indicates you have work to do.[8]

FINDING—AND DELIVERING—YOUR BRAND

You can have a strong brand. In fact, you may already have one, but didn't know that that's what it's called.

Now, I have to admit that no law says you *must* worry about long-term brand equity. Marketing history, direct marketing history in particular, is full of flash-in-the-pan products—like the Ginsu knife, Abdomenizer, Smokeless Ashtray, Pet Rock, and others—that sold oodles, and generated record profits, with little regard for the long haul. So, if you want to capitalize on a momentarily open window, you can.

But marketers, even direct marketers, who want to prosper for the long haul, need staying power, because windows close, fads pass, and knockoffs arise. And the foundation of staying power is found in the brand, even for those who sell by mail, by phone, or online.

Chances are the makings of a strong brand already exist within your company or within the minds of its leadership. The trick is to discover your brand, develop it, live it, and ensure its delivery at every point of contact.

This will require, among other things, leadership. Posters in the break room and ads in the paper saying "Customers come first" fall flat when the CEO plays hermit. Branding begins at the top. Values trickle down, never up.

If you need help discovering and delivering on your brand, there are many fine firms, including some ad agencies, that can help. A good one will push your organization on how it delivers on its promises first, and deal with expressing them second.

But please beware any agency or consultant that offers to give you a brand or rebrand wrapped up in a slogan and a logo.

With your brand in place, your ad agency can get to work. Whether you give them objectives for building brand awareness, selling products, or both, they will be able to build their work on a solid foundation, and elegantly and substantively promote your brand in the process.

SUMMARY POINTS FROM
A CRITICAL LOOK AT BRANDING

- All advertising, including direct response, affects the brand.

- The brand affects direct response.

- A logo, a graphic look, and a tagline do not make a brand.

- A brand is the values that you, your company, and your people *live*.

- While shallow branding tactics may have worked in the past, today's consumers demand substance.

- If you masked your logo, would your customers know you from the competition?

- Would your customers jilt you for a lower-priced look-alike?

- Does anyone besides you believe what your advertising claims? (Come on. Be honest.)

- Do your core values *really* set you apart from competitors?

- Do you and your employees know what you stand for? And do they stand with you?

- You have a brand. It may be strong or weak, but you have one. The trick is to uncover it. And, if need be, refine it, strengthen it, and recommit to it.

- Advertising is just one of many avenues through which you communicate your brand.

7

BEWARE THE EXPERTS

Crowd enough people into a room, and you may be surprised at how many of them share a birthday.

You may be less surprised, however, when you think it through. Allowing for leap years, all it takes to *guarantee* a match is 367 people. But there's no need for so many. A 1996 study by statisticians Persi Diaconis and Frederick Mosteller[1] shows that in a random selection of 23 people, there's a 50 percent chance of at least two matched birthdays.[2]

That brings us to the Law of Truly Large Numbers, a term statisticians use when the rest of us would have said "coincidence." In *The Skeptic's Dictionary: A Collection of Strange Beliefs, Amusing Deceptions, and Dangerous Delusions*, Robert Todd Carroll explains the Law of Truly Large Numbers this way: "With a large enough sample, many seeming unlikely coincidences are *likely* to happen." Repeatedly throw M&Ms on the floor, and sometimes the reds and yellows will land in clusters. Talk to enough people with premonitions, and some of them will turn out to be right more often than the average. Expose enough people with cancer to daily doses of positive thinking, and some of them will go into remission. Expose enough toddlers to Mozart, and some of them will turn out to have above-average intelligence. It may appear tempting to resist passing off such occurrences as coincidence. But in a world with over six billion people, even an occurrence with million-to-one odds against it isn't just possible, but is *likely* to happen 6,000 times. In fact, it's nearly impossible that it *wouldn't* happen. In our world, a miracle would be a *lack* of amazing coincidences.

Marketers may not be as plentiful as M&Ms, premonitions, or New Age cures, but there are more than enough of them making gut-based rather than carefully tested and validated decisions every day for the Law of Truly Large Numbers to kick in. A certain number of these gut-based decisions will inevitably score. Not only that. Some are bound to score again and again.

The Law of Truly Large Numbers also allows for a certain number of marketers following their gut-level intuition to stumble upon a genuine winning formula. Good for them. It's the others I'm worried about. As long as their luck holds, they will assume they too have a winning formula.[3] When their luck ceases, many will disqualify the cessation, defend and make excuses for their methods, and stubbornly throw perfectly good marketing money after bad.

Marketers who make a habit of counting successes and disqualifying failures will grow convinced of their formulas and may eventually become consultants, going on to put other companies in harm's way for outrageous fees.

Worse, some of *them* will go on to write books, or to have books written about them. And here we return to the Law of Truly Large Numbers, which tells us there's a good chance that some of those books will become best sellers, putting even more companies in harm's way for the price of a book plus tax.

SUITABLY JAUNDICED EYE

I am not calling books about marketing worthless. On the contrary, I am a fan of marketing books, and I devour as many as I can as fast as I can. Many, if not most, offer useful information, insights, and gems of thought.

But I *do* suggest reading them with caution. Marketing books tend to blend, in varying ratios, the scholarly with the evangelical. They back hypotheses with data of varying degrees of reliability to create an appearance of science and, in doses ranging from subtle to shameless, convince unsuspecting readers using tactics much like cheerleading. The combination of pseudoscience and motivational persuasion can be convincing, and that can be dangerous. It's one thing to search books for ideas worth trying out. It's quite another to accept them as the Marketing Authority.

A variety of winning formulas can be found in the marketing and advertising sections of any bookstore. In this chapter I take on three in particular. I call the first one the *Exemplar Fallacy*, which assumes that the practices of a successful person or company can be identified and adapted to the sure success of another. The second one is the *Overriding Principle Fallacy*, which attempts to prove a single practice as the key to business success based on its presence in other successful companies and absence in struggling ones.

The third is the *Scholarly Spectrum Fallacy*—a laundry list of practices across an array of successful companies that is presumed to account for their success and held to be all that stands between your company and Fortune 500 status.

All three genres recur with regularity and frequency under new titles, covers, and authors, which attests to their popularity and power. All the more reason to invoke critical thinking and read with a suitably jaundiced eye before canonizing one as your corporate owner's manual.

THE EXEMPLAR FALLACY

On April 12, 2004, Ashley Revell entered the Plaza Hotel in Las Vegas, walked up to a roulette wheel, and bet every cent to his name on red. The ball landed on Red 7. Revell, having doubled his $135,300, then performed his first intelligent act of the day. He took his money and left.

Few people would argue that Revell was wise to try such a stunt. Assuming a balanced wheel and a fair flick of the croupier's wrist, Revell's odds of winning—and losing—were a terrifying less than one in two. From a statistical standpoint, the potential winnings hardly stood up against the risk of total ruin. If the Revell who bet all on red took an unwise risk, certainly the Revell who walked away a moment later with $270,600 had taken no less of one.

Now imagine if Ashley Revell wrote a how-to book on doubling your holdings. "Timing is important," the book might advise. "I suggest gambling on Monday night, as I did. Dress matters, too. I felt strongly that wearing a rented—not purchased—tux would increase my odds and, well, you saw what happened as a result. Most important, be sure to bet everything you own, and bet it all on *red*. Red gives off more positive energy than black. I knew that if I had bet on black, I'd have lost it all."

Nonsense, I hope you say. We all know that Revell's choices of time, tux, and red had no impact on his odds. We know that holding up Revell as an exemplar would be unwise.

Or do we? Let's look at a few marketing books that indulge the Exemplar Fallacy.

We have *Think like a Billionaire: Everything You Need to Know about Success, Real Estate, and Life*. That would certainly seem to cover the gamut. But wait. Here's *How to Get Rich*, which is even more to the point. And one more: *The Art of the Deal*. Each of these titles, by the way, is ostensibly written by Donald Trump with the aid of a co-author. Read these books and you will learn what made Donald Trump Donald Trump, and, it seems, how to become Donald Trump yourself. If you don't believe it, read the front flap of *Think like a Billionaire*: "It's not good enough to want it. You've got to know how to get it . . . Donald J. Trump is the man to teach you . . . crucial advice from the expert . . . how to impress anyone . . . everything you need to know to get ahead." There you have it. With all the finesse of a nineteenth-century patent medicine ad, Trump sells a cure for financial woes.

Other titles promise equally miraculous insights for bolstering your business. There's *Make Winning a Habit—20 Best Practices of the World's Greatest Sales Forces* by Rick Page. According to ComplexSale.com, this book reveals how "five universal areas of sales effectiveness" overlapped with "the four levels of sales strategy" result in "twenty sales best practices that will make success more than a quota-by-quota occurrence [*sic*]."

At the extreme end are books like *Leadership Secrets of Attila the Hun* and *Napoleon on Project Management*. These are not so much analyses as analogies. In reality, they are not management gems at all. They are a creative attempt at capitalizing on an attention-getting title and concept that can't be developed into anything substantive.

Yet, much like my facetiously proposed Ashley Revell method, each of the titles mentioned here would have readers believe that one person or company—one exemplar—represents a valid sample, and that a look at selected behaviors of that exemplar will unlock secrets of success.

"IF ROGER DID IT . . ."

There was a time when it was impossible for humans to run a mile in four minutes. Until, that is, Roger Bannister did it in 1954. Suddenly, everyone knew it was possible, after all. If Roger could do it, so could anyone else.

The only problem? It's simply not true. A better statement would be, "If Roger could do it, so could *others*." Not *everyone*. Whether due to physical, emotional, or mental limitations, some people, even at gunpoint, simply cannot run a mile at all, much less in four minutes.

Yet inspirational marketing stories designed to cajole us into thinking we can run a four-minute mile continue popping up.

Take Jeff Bezos, who put Amazon.com together in a matter of weeks. He chose to open an Internet business upon seeing the Web's explosive, 2,300 percent growth in 1994. Settling on books as a good online product, Bezos decided to locate his new business in the western United States, where computer technology seemed to be making its home. He chose Seattle and sent the movers on their way. Seated on the passenger side of the car while his wife drove them west, Bezos tapped out a business plan on his laptop computer. What one popular marketing book suggests is to be learned from this is that one more moment's delay or forethought might have ruined the whole thing. Don't delay, urges the book; just act. It worked for Bezos; therefore, it will work for you.

But . . . will it? Besides seeing an opportunity and not letting grass grow, Bezos had a few other factors working in his favor. Like the way his mind works, personal circumstances that allowed him to quit one enterprise and launch another, a supportive spouse, personal charm, keen business sense—and let's not forget *timing*. Without the convergence of events that provided fertile ground for his new enterprise, much less the prior invention of the Internet, Bezos might never have launched anything. Unlike making the quick decision to head west and write a business plan en route, these factors are not so easily duplicated.

We also have no way of knowing if Bezos would have been more or less successful had he taken longer and planned harder. All we know is that things worked out for him. But that doesn't mean that because Bezos did it, so can you. Nor does it mean that his success establishes a guaranteed formula if others will only use it.

I chuckled when I read a business book with a chapter focusing on Bill Gates. Its postulate was that if you understand and reenact what Gates did, you will succeed. If Gates did it, so can you.

There's no arguing that Gates is a rather successful entrepreneur, that his success is well deserved, and that the man is brilliant. But the same Bill Gates with the same gifts and drive might not have accomplished anything remarkable had he been born before computers were invented, in a country without electricity, or in a remote rural farming community where it was assumed he would someday take over the family farm. Sometimes environment matters. Sometimes, as in the case of Ashley Revell, *happenstance* matters.

Doing what Roger Bannister, Jeff Bezos, or Bill Gates did does not ensure you will have the same outcome, even if you follow the same steps.[4] Not unless you can also duplicate their minds, talents, environments, partners, opportunities, and good fortune. It's better to learn what you can from their positive examples, build your own plan, and test, test, test.[5]

THE OVERRIDING PRINCIPLE FALLACY

Every now and then a marketer notes a common trait among two or more successful marketers and begins to wonder if there's more to it than coincidence. That's a valid question, but researching it can be tricky, because when you know the conclusion you wish to draw and go looking for evidence to support it, you risk falling victim to *selection bias*.[6] If you're not careful, you end up not with an overriding principle, but committing the Overriding Principle Fallacy.

A number of marketing books have done exactly that.

Suppose, for instance, you noticed that 7-Up gained recognition by positioning itself as *not* a cola, Avis grew its market share by positioning itself as the second-place car rental agency, and Jeep maintained recognition by exploiting its position as the original SUV. You might decide that positioning your product vis-à-vis a reference point in consumer minds is the overriding principle when it comes to marketing success. To defend your point, you might research other successful products with similar positioning strategies and unsuccessful products without. When you find enough of each, you might write a book called *Positioning: The Battle for Your Mind*.

Or suppose you notice successful companies that refine their focus to a narrow niche. You might decide that focusing is the overriding principle, and *prove* it by contrasting highly successful, single-focus companies with less successful, diversified companies. Then you could write a book called *Focus: The Future of Your Company Depends on It*.

But let me save you some trouble. Your first problem will be that starting with a conclusion and digging to support it isn't science. Science starts with a hypothesis as suggested by exhaustive evidence, followed by careful testing, rigorous controls, and full consideration for alternate explanations. You can't prove that *position* or *focus* is causal unless you can prove that all other factors (and combinations of factors) aren't.

Notwithstanding, you'd probably end up writing a compelling book, a good read with plenty of useful information that any marketer worth his or her salt should devour and consider. But you'd be too late. Al Ries, writing sometimes on his own, sometimes with co-author Jack Trout or Laura Ries, beat you to the first, the second, and a complement of other books.

In fairness, Ries et al. make easy pickings because of the sheer volume of titles to their credit. But others, like *Whatever You Think, Think the Opposite*, by Paul Arden, abound.[7] I should add that, like other intelligent business volumes, such books can be useful, even inspiring. But it is important not to mistake the Overriding Principle Fallacy, no matter how well defended by myriad examples it may appear to be, as *conclusive*. At best, and at its most useful, it is *suggestive*.

AN EXCELLENT SEARCH FOR GREATNESS: THE SCHOLARLY SPECTRUM FALLACY

In 1982, the book *In Search of Excellence* became what was at the time a rarity among business books: a runaway best seller.

In a scholarly attempt to find what made certain companies hugely successful, authors Thomas J. Peters and Robert H. Waterman Jr. didn't settle for profiling one company, person, or method. Rather, they examined 62 publicly traded companies against six performance-based standards. The standards included years in business (a minimum of 20), asset growth, equity growth, book-to-market value, return on capital investment, and average return on investment. Peters and Waterman deemed companies meeting any four of the six standards "excellent." These companies were then subjected to scrutiny in search of commonly held practices. Presumably, the commonality would provide a blueprint other companies could follow to excellence of their own.

When all was said and done, Peters and Waterman concluded that "excellent" companies tended to have a "bias for action"; stayed "close to the customer"; fostered "autonomy and entrepreneurship"; effected "productivity through people"; believed in "hands-on" and "value-added" approaches; stuck "to the knitting"; maintained a "simple form" with a "lean staff"; and held to "simultaneous loose-tight properties," that is, stronger controls through giving plenty of leash.

In Search of Excellence was an instant hit. It became scripture for managers throughout the United States, providing chapter and verse for anyone who wanted to defend or challenge a management practice.[8, 9]

An inevitable reincarnation of *In Search of Excellence* appeared in 2001, in the form of the book *Good to Great* by Jim Collins. In hauntingly familiar fashion, Collins weighed public companies against his own laundry list of performance-based criteria: 15 years of cumulative stock return at or above par, performance outstripping both industry standards and "comparison companies," and others.

Collins's findings among companies meeting the criteria for *greatness* included a tendency to choose *who* before *what*; the ability to confront "brutal facts"; the "Hedgehog Principle," which, despite the author's denial, was "stick to the knitting" in a new suit of clothes; maintaining a "culture of discipline"; remaining technologically adept; and taking a slow and steady approach.

Like its earlier incarnation, *Good to Great* became a best seller and the new manual for success. The implication and rallying cry was that doing what Collins found "great" companies do would lead your own company to prosperity.

Both books are great reads, filled with insights worth pondering, perhaps even implementing, in any enterprise. Both books take a scholarly approach. No one would argue the authors failed to do their homework, or that they failed to present and defend their cases.

But a scholarly work isn't necessarily a scientific one. Under scrutiny, it becomes clear that books like *In Search of Excellence*, *Good to Great*, and others like them fall short of providing the business person's panacea.

ELUSIVE EXCELLENCE AND GREATNESS

Suppose we really wanted to learn what makes successful companies successful. If you're Peters and Waterman, that means you're going to have to define *excellent*. If you're Collins, you're going to have to define *great*.

That's a problem. *Excellent* and *great* are subjective terms. The authors arbitrarily defined qualifying criteria. Who's to say that equity growth, being publicly traded, or years in business really are valid measures of excellence? What about potential qualifiers the authors omitted, like brand preference, employee longevity, or diminishing cost per sale? Perhaps the authors adopted some wrong criteria or omitted some right ones.

But let's assume the authors correctly nailed what qualifies a company as excellent or great. Next comes the task of detecting exactly what those companies did that made them so. The authors searched for practices that qualifying companies held in common, the assumption being that the traits those companies share account for their success.

This may be a compelling argument, even an appealing one, but it's also erroneous. Arbitrariness must once again be invoked to determine which shared traits matter and which don't. It's all well and good to note that the studied companies all seem to "stick to the knitting" and show a "bias for action." But doubtless a little digging would uncover other shared traits, such as restroom cleanliness standards, tuition reimbursement programs, commitment to equal opportunity, employee newsletters, sound marketing strategies, well-executed advertising campaigns, policies for dealing with vendors, and myriad other factors. Why omit these factors when considering what makes the studied companies successful?[10]

A study of *unsuccessful* companies might also enlighten. Knowing that no unsuccessful company shared the identified practices would go a long way toward validating the authors' success determiners. On the other hand, a good representation of failed companies meeting the criteria would undo their conclusions.[11]

There are other problems with the Scholarly Spectrum. Searching for commonality among Disney, Wendy's, Chrysler, and Kentucky Fried Chicken could lead to the conclusion that featuring your CEO in advertising is a panacea. A look at Nike, Coca-Cola, or any fashion advertiser in the pages of *Vogue* magazine might tell you that all it takes for successful advertising is dramatic imagery and a logo. And a look at Martha Stewart, Bill Clinton, or Paris Hilton could be used to establish that public scandal strengthens celebrity.

Traits that successful companies share do not establish a recipe for success. At best, they establish models worthy of consideration. At worst, they represent naught but the Law of Truly Large Numbers in action.

THE BUSINESS FORTUNE-TELLER

Taking another look at the authors' conclusions themselves is instructive. For all their research, the advice we're left with is remarkably mundane.[12] Choosing action over inaction, staying close to the customer, keeping things simple, encouraging discipline, embracing technology, and sticking to what you're good at are not exactly earth-shattering, breakthrough attributes. Many companies could arguably claim them.

And that can beguile the business owner in the same way a psychic beguiles a mark. If you want to convince people you're a psychic, tell them things that are likely to apply to just about anyone. Try something like, "You're flexible, but you know when to put your foot down. You're patient, but there are times your temper flares. You have been thinking about a journey. You either met someone recently or will meet someone soon who will change the course of your life." Within moments, your subject will be nodding in enthusiastic agreement. Many business books offer equally claimable, universally applicable principles— which may explain their immediate appeal. Because they could apply to anyone, it's an easy matter to read either volume, pat yourself on the back, and tell yourself you're doing just fine.

Perhaps this is why, upon the publication of *In Search of Excellence* and later of *Good to Great*, many companies, instead of looking for ways to improve, chose to feel validated instead. The principles in both books are at once ubiquitous and imprecise, such that nearly anyone can claim to abide by them with little or no self-deception.

None of this is to say you shouldn't read *In Search of Excellence, Good to Great*, or other like volumes. They brim with great ideas. They motivate. They inspire.

Just don't mistake them for the Final Word.

THE INSTANT EXPERT

Attorneys may face difficulties with their local bar association for claiming to be *experts* in a given field. To the Bar Association's credit, an attorney must meet strict criteria to justify making such a claim. Similarly, there are stringent requirements one must fill before legally claiming to be a medical doctor, a dentist, a pilot, or an engineer. But most professions aren't so stringent. So before concluding this chapter, let me add a word about what it usually takes to set yourself up as an expert. Often, there are only two requirements:

1. Leave home. Matthew 13:57 says, "A prophet is not without honor, save in his own country, and in his own house." There's something compelling about a woman or man who hops on a plane and travels to a destination where people pay for her or his opinions. But always remember that, back home, that person goes by a first name, usually preceded by "just."

2. Be dogmatic. Argument from Authority, which I address elsewhere in this book, is compelling, and it's human nature to be swayed by someone who assumes an authoritative persona. But Argument from Authority is a logical fallacy, namely because authorities can make mistakes.

There are experts and there are experts. Some are more consistently reliable than others. Most if not all have at least something to offer. So I'm not suggesting discarding every piece of advice. What I'm suggesting is that you carefully engage your own critical thinking as you weigh their advice.

Devour every marketing book you can find and lap up what the consultants pour out. But no matter how reasonable, appealing, or compelling an argument, don't simply assume it's right. Use your head.

In short, don't trust everything you read in a book.

Not even this one.

SUMMARY POINTS FROM
BEWARE THE EXPERTS

- With large numbers, unlikely coincidences happen.

- Therefore it's easy to mistake luck for expertise.

- You should listen to and profit from experts, but it's a good precaution to develop and maintain a skeptical eye.

- Good scholarship and good science aren't the same thing.

- Beware the Exemplar Fallacy. Doing what the likes of Jeff Bezos or Bill Gates do doesn't mean you'll end up with the next Amazon.com or Microsoft.

(Continued)

- No one really knows conclusively what makes the likes of Jeff Bezos or Bill Gates successful, anyway.

- Many business books rely on the Overriding Principle Fallacy, whose formulas for success are little more than an exercise in selection bias.

- Compiling traits that multiple successful companies appear to have in common commits the Scholarly Spectrum Fallacy. It does not necessarily explain their success and will not ensure yours.

- Fortune-tellers amaze people by telling them things that, upon examination, could apply to anyone. Much business advice is the same. Do you really need a high-priced expert's massive research and experience to tell you to hire carefully and focus on core capabilities?

- Business books are a great source for tips and inspiration. But do not mistake them for science.

- Don't trust every book you read. Including this one.

8

HELP STOP RESEARCH ABUSE

A friend with an immensely successful restaurant decided it was time to build another one. When people in one focus group after another promised to shower him with cash for selling his legendary burgers a little closer to home, he opened the new location. That was 20 years ago. The place is still losing money.

Not too long ago, focus groups made it abundantly clear that Herman Miller Inc.'s new Aeron office chair would fail. It became a top seller.

A client wanted to know what would make more people subscribe to his publication. I suggested a strong gift offer, which is a proven tactic for publishers. He hesitated. The research firm he hired had just phoned 500 prospective subscribers who said that gift offers would fail to win their business. But when we tested two versions of the mailing—one with a gift offer, the other without—the gift offer version sold 20 percent more.

And in the weeks leading up to the U.S. presidential election of 1948, the esteemed Gallup and Roper polls both produced statistically valid data showing that Dewey was going to utterly trounce Truman.[1]

RESEARCH HERESY

I'm not going to tell you that qualitative research from focus groups and quantitative research from phone and Internet surveys are a crock. On the contrary, they can be useful. They can reveal contingencies, potential pitfalls, potential opportunities, and ideas to explore. They can tell you a good deal about people's self-concepts, prejudices, and behaviors.

But there is one thing that neither qualitative nor quantitative research cannot do: namely, predict behavior.

I realize that to many I am committing nothing short of research heresy. I ask that you set aside the tar and feathers long enough for a commonsense look at human psychology, along with some revealing neurological findings. I intend to show you that we are better at fooling ourselves than we ever thought, and even better at fooling even the most astute researchers.

LEARNING TO PLEASE

We grow up learning to please.

In school, we learn to pass tests by giving the answer the teacher wants, not the one we believe. My English teachers marked students down for writing short paragraphs, while my journalism teachers marked us down for writing long ones. It wasn't until after graduation that I developed my own rule for paragraph length.[2]

At home, we learn to answer questions to stay out of trouble. Every child knows that the proper response to

"Who put the fork in the garbage disposal?" is "I don't know." If you're the culprit, "I don't know" might spare you a scolding. If a sibling or friend is the culprit, "I don't know" might spare you a tattler label along with possible bodily harm.

When we begin dating, we say whatever it takes to appeal to the moment's object of our affection. I still shudder at the memory of telling my high school girlfriend I liked her yappy little poodles.

Even as adults, many of us skew our own self-talk toward what we like to believe about ourselves. Old men who flirt with young women tell themselves they're not cads, they're young at heart. People with weight problems tell themselves they're big boned or have a slow metabolism. People fired for cause tell themselves their employer was out to get them.

KIDDING OURSELVES

After a lifetime of failing to level with others and ourselves, it's hard for any of us to know what we really think. No wonder many people undergo years of monthly sessions with experienced mental health professionals in search of self-honesty—and a large number never attain it.

Out-of-touch-with-oneself-ness isn't limited to people in therapy. Consider how many times, after a conversation with co-workers, friends, or family, you've walked away thinking, "These people are just kidding themselves."

If that many of us have that much trouble sorting out our own thoughts and feelings, ask yourself how reasonable it is to expect people in a focus group or survey to be able to tell you anything insightful about their motivations, preferences, or inclinations. Ask yourself how accurately they can predict their own choices in hypothetical buying decisions. Ask yourself how reasonable it is to ask people to predict—with any degree of accuracy—the marketing approach, color, package, headline, layout, or concept most likely to make them buy. Though respondents will do their best to give you a helpful answer, the fact is, they haven't a clue.

In his book *How Customers Think: Essential Insights into the Mind of the Market*, Harvard Business School professor of marketing Gerald Zaltman cites a study in which survey respondents' answers varied depending on the order in which survey questions were asked. Some even varied with the color of paper on which the survey was printed.

Perhaps, then, you can see the problem with research cited in the book *Selling the Invisible: A Field Guide to Modern Marketing*, by Harry Beckwith, in which respondents were shown two commercials for the same model of car. One commercial focused on the car's performance; the other enumerated the car's features. When researchers asked, "If either commercial might make them switch to that brand of car," 6 percent said the more focused spot would make them change, while none voted for the feature-oriented spot.[3] From this, Beckwith concludes that advertising should focus on a single product attribute, and that a list of features is counterproductive. It's a popular, but not a reliable notion. For one thing, context suggests that Beckwith set out to reach that very conclusion. If so, confirmation and selection bias were all but inevitable. For another, there is ample evidence that contradicts it.[4] But, most important for present purposes, Beckwith fails to note that *people cannot accurately predict or explain their own behavior*.

The fact that too many researchers overlook or ignore is that, whenever you ask anyone a direct question, you encounter a serious problem.

THE DIRECT QUESTION PROBLEM

One of my clients recently hired a research firm to find out why people buy a certain product. I cringed when I learned the research firm based its conclusions—and recommendations—on asking a large sample of customers direct questions about why they buy.

To illustrate why direct questions fail to produce usable data, consider this research question: When you visit a casino, how do you decide which one-armed bandit to play?

Unless you follow the literature on this particular bit of trivia, I'd be surprised if you know the real answer. I'd even be surprised if you *think* you know. But there is evidence that bright colors—reds and purples, for instance—draw people to a bank of slots, while blues and greens tend to keep them playing. So savvy casino designers place the bright colors on the ends of a row of slot machines, and place the more muted-colored machines inside. People passing by tend to pause at an end machine, but move toward the center machines to linger, which in turn frees the outer machines to attract new players.[5]

I can assure you that phoning 5,000 Las Vegas enthusiasts and asking them a direct question like the one I just asked you would never have produced this information. Not too many slot players would respond, "I'm attracted to purple, but then I settle down with the earth tones." The gaming industry picked up this information by other means.[6]

LEFT BRAINS TELL STORIES

In *The Blank Slate: The Modern Denial of Human Nature*, author and head of Harvard University's psychology department Steven Pinker describes fascinating experiments with people whose brain hemispheres had been surgically separated. (The procedure is sometimes helpful for stroke victims.)

Severed brain halves cannot communicate with each other, which presents opportunities to gain insights about the functions of each half. Because the right eye connects to the left brain and the left eye to the right, it's possible to cover one eye and present a written command to the corresponding brain hemisphere while, amazingly, the *other* half of the split brain remains oblivious.

Such experiments have revealed that the left brain is quite the storyteller. For instance, if you tell such a split-brain subject's *right* brain to walk, Pinker explains, the subject will stand up to do so. But something interesting happens when you stop the subject and ask the *left* brain, "Why did you stand up?" You might expect the left brain, with no knowledge of the command, to answer, "I don't know." But it turns out that left brains don't admit things like that. Instead, the left brain will fabricate an answer, like, "To get a drink." And mean it.[7]

This isn't unique. The extremely creative left brain would rather say anything than, "I don't know"—and it does. A left brain that lacks information invents it, and the brain's owner doesn't know the difference.

The left brain works no less diligently supplying rationalizations when fully connected to the right. Pinker writes, "The spooky part is that we have no reason to think that the baloney-generator in the patient's left hemisphere is behaving any differently from ours as we make sense of the inclinations emanating from the rest of our brains. The conscious mind—the self or soul—is a spin doctor."[8,9]

If you are a researcher, the implication is clear. You cannot trust the answer to any survey question that opens with, "Why do you . . . ?," "What do you . . . ?," "What would you do if . . . ?," or "Which would you prefer?"

SMART RESEARCHERS

The research field does have its share of brilliant professionals who know how to ferret out good information and separate it from bad.

In his book *Ogilvy on Advertising*, David Ogilvy relates an experience from his days as a researcher for the Gallup Organization, when *Gone with the Wind* was a bestseller. Ogilvy's assignment was to find out how many people had actually read the book. After too many positive answers to the direct question, "Have you read *Gone with the Wind*?", Ogilvy made the subtle but brilliant change to, "Do you plan to read *Gone With the Wind*?". Having provided respondents a way to admit not having read the book and still save face, false positive answers dropped dramatically.

Research expert Justin Ethington of Volt Marketing in Salt Lake City told me about another savvy maneuver for getting closer to the truth. His client wanted to use a focus group to find out if women would pay $20 for the client's product. Ethington objected that focus group research couldn't accurately answer that question, but the client insisted. Overwhelmingly, women assured researchers that they would pay $20 for the product. The client was ready to start printing $20 price tags when Ethington added a cagey follow-up question: "If you had only twenty dollars to spend and you had to choose between this product and a pair of shoes, which would you buy?" Every woman in the sample said she would cheerfully give up the product and buy the shoes.

I once consulted for a pest extermination company. Their direct-question research showed that advertising's chief message should be that their service ensured the safety of children and pets. I was unconvinced, so we conducted our own research. When we asked people to rank possible advertising claims, sure enough, most placed child and pet safety at the top. But when we asked people to rank what they thought mattered to their neighbors, nearly all said, "They want to know if you guarantee killing the bugs." What about child and pet safety? Respondents said, "People assume they'll be safe." For our client, the exercise was an eye-opener. It didn't reveal what to claim in their advertising. What it revealed was that answers change depending on how questions are posed. It became clear to our client that they would not learn how to advertise extermination services simply by asking people their thoughts.

HELP STOP RESEARCH ABUSE

Not all researchers are as savvy as an Ethington or Ogilvy. Because research methods *appear* easy to imitate, the profession attracts its share of less competent practitioners. Unless you have solid research background yourself, it can be hard to tell one from the other, but here's a good starting point: The moment you're asked to rely on the results of research that asks people to explain or predict their own behavior, you're dealing with research abuse.

Many companies hold focus groups. They fill a room with 10 to 20 carefully selected respondents and ask them questions. That much is fine. A problem occurs only when companies mistake the resultant *feedback* for *data*—and make decisions based on what they hear.

Focus groups, with an easy-to-imitate format, are a great place for incompetents to convince themselves and unsuspecting clients that they know what they're doing.

Anyone can convene a group, ask questions, and write up the answers.

I have seen focus group reports that say things like, "Seventy percent felt the packaging was too pink" or "Eighty percent said if you open a store on the West Side, they'll shop there." I have seen the people running the focus groups, whose role is to remain unbiased, ask leading questions like, "Would you be more or less likely to shop at a store that advertises on violent cartoons aimed at small children?"

Amazingly and sadly, businesses actually base big decisions on these groups. They make the package less pink. They open a store on the West Side. They pull their ads from Batman cartoons. And all too often they later find that consumers don't behave the way they said they would in the focus group.

Telebrands founder A. J. Kubani experienced this phenomenon firsthand when focus group participants assured him they would unhesitatingly fork over $19.99 for a mop product called Robo-Maid. Kubani had a supply of the product on hand, which he offered to sell them then and there. None of the participants bought. Later, Robo-Maid failed in the marketplace.[10] The *behavior* of the focus group participants, not their *answers*, turned out to be predictive.

Don't get me wrong. I am not against focus groups themselves. What I'm against is the *misuse* of focus groups. A focus group doesn't and can't yield quantitative, statistically valid research. It's a great place to get insights and suggestions. Not marching orders.

What focus groups *can* do is raise ideas, options, and contingencies you hadn't considered. You can emerge from a focus group with a wealth of information you might not have considered on your own. Focus groups can also teach you a lot about how dominant personalities influence others—even when participants write their answers before sharing them aloud.[11, 12] But the moment someone begins summarizing focus group data as percentages—"seventy percent of participants prefer lime to blueberry"—or using it to generalize or predict buying habits, watch out. You're dealing with research abuse.

Quantitative research—large-scale surveys by mail, e-mail, Web, telephone, and so forth—can be statistically significant and reliable, provided respondents are selected from the right markets, questions are properly crafted, and the folks analyzing the data know their right hands from their left. Quantitative research can reveal what people know. It can reveal what they remember. Carefully crafted, it can reveal opinions, biases, and a wealth of information about respondents' self-concepts.

But this, too, has its limits. People don't know—or care to admit—what section of the newspaper they read first. They don't know why they prefer one brand over another. And they have no clue whether they'd buy more of your product if you moved it closer to the cereal aisle or put a jingle on the radio.

I recently met with an executive who avowed that she *never* responds to direct mail, that none of her customers respond to it, and that to send her customers direct mail would be an insult. I know this is untrue from years of mailing to upscale people. By sheer happenstance, I also happened to know (but couldn't reveal) that this particular executive receives direct mail from one of our clients and responds to it regularly. I do not accuse her of lying; I accuse her of being human. She honestly has no clue how she behaves in the marketplace. Experience shows that she represents the norm. You should take that into consideration before phoning 5,000 people to ask about their buying habits.

ANOTHER APPROACH TO RESEARCH

None of this is news to skilled, responsible researchers. The good ones know that self-honesty and inner motivators are elusive, and they don't try to get research to do what it cannot. But not all researchers are skilled or responsible, which is why it behooves all marketers to understand what qualitative and quantitative research can and can't do.

Now for some good news. There is a way to find out, before you plunk down a large sum, how your marketing will work. It's *another* approach to research that we haven't talked about yet. For reasons beyond me, it is largely ignored by most marketers, yet it is the most reliable, accurate predictor of market behavior available.

Even better, it's not that hard or even costly to do.

In fact, it's so good, I'm going to give it its own chapter.

SUMMARY POINTS FROM
HELP STOP RESEARCH ABUSE

- Qualitative and quantitative research (respectively, focus groups and phone, mail, and Internet surveys) cannot predict consumer behavior. To expect them to do so is research abuse.

- Don't bother asking people what they think, what they tend to do, why they do it, or what they would do in a hypothetical situation. They haven't a clue.

- People are trained to give the "right" answer, not the real one.

(Continued)

- It's human nature not to know when we're kidding ourselves.

- Neurological tests on patients with split brains reveal that people unknowingly fool themselves all the time.

- All of this has serious implications for research. To make decisions based on verbal feedback from even a large sample of people is foolhardy.

- Some researchers are skilled at digging out hidden information. They are rare gems, but even the insights they ferret out cannot reliably predict market behavior.

- Good news: There *is* a way to predict market behavior, and you don't need a researcher or a huge budget to do it. (See Chapter 9)

9

HOW TO PREDICT A MARKETING SUCCESS

What do you think would be likely to happen if you were to: (a) sneak up and yell at someone lost in thought?; (b) tell a funny joke?; (c) wear formal attire to a video arcade?

I think we can agree there's a high likelihood that: (a) the person will jump; (b) people will laugh; (c) people will stare.

Predicting these reactions isn't hard. Each of us has seen what happens when people are startled, jokes are told, and people look out of place. We've seen it so often that we know what to expect.

And *that* is the key to valid, predictive research. When most people react repeatedly to the same situation in the same way, we can predict with a high degree of reliability that, next time, most people will react to the same situation in exactly the same way.

PREDICTABLE US

It doesn't take extremes like jumping from the shadows and yelling "Boo!" to bring out predictable human behavior. Our species is far more consistent than most of us realize.

We eat more when we see reds and yellows. We're more likely to clean our plate if the plate has a pattern on it.[1]

We open envelopes with the back facing us.

Right-handed people look up and right when lying or improvising, up and left when recalling. Left-handed people do the opposite.

We start diets in January. We watch less TV in summer.

We take our kids to the dentist in July and August. People with flex plans crowd in dentist and doctor visits at year-end.

NEVER HIT A CUSTOMER WITH A PHOTON

Consistent behaviors in humans can be useful to marketers who are smart enough to identify and capitalize on those behaviors. It's no accident that fast food places like McDonald's, Burger King, Wendy's, Carl's Jr., and Pizza Hut sport reds and yellows in their signs, interiors, and packaging. Nor is it accidental that miracle diets are promoted most heavily (no pun intended) in January, nor that direct mail marketers are picky about the order in which contents are stuffed in their envelopes.

The challenge comes in knowing consistent from capricious behavior. By now, I hope you agree that it's naïve and futile to *ask* people how they behave. You'll get nowhere asking 5,000 people if yellow and red inspire them to eat more.

If you want to find out how your customers are going to behave, there is only one reliable way to do it, and that is *to observe them yourself in the real world.* When you see people respond consistently over time in the same way to the same ad, display, color, packaging, scent, layout, headline, web banner, point-of-purchase device, or what have you, chances are you have a reliable indicator for predicting ongoing behavior.

But there is a catch, analogous to the Heisenberg Uncertainty Principle in physics. A physicist who wants to observe a subatomic particle must first illuminate it. The trouble is that illuminating a particle requires hitting it with photons, and hitting a particle with photons will change its behavior in the form of sending it off in a new direction. This makes it difficult if not impossible to know how particles behave when you're *not* bombarding them with photons—that is, when you're not watching them.

Figuratively speaking, the behavior of people also changes when you shine a light on them.[2] If they know someone is watching, their behavior changes, as the following joke illustrates:

Q: Why should you never go fishing with fewer than two people who are morally opposed to alcohol?

A: If you take just one, you'll end up having to share your beer.[3]

When people think that no one is watching, they're more likely to let down their guard and show their natural behavior. Consider what politicians say when the microphones are off—that is, when they think they're off— versus their guarded statements when they know the microphones are on. Consider the number of men who won't enter the adult section of a magazine shop without first looking over their shoulders. Consider how much better hourly employees are at holding their breaks to fifteen minutes when they know the boss is timing them.

So for reliable data on customer behavior, you must observe your customers with strict adherence to two conditions:

1. Your customers must be acting in the real world, not a laboratory simulation.

2. Your customers must not know a test is under way or that you're even watching. Otherwise, you will undo the effect of observing them in the real world.

WATCHING CUSTOMERS FOR FUN AND PROFIT

Suppose you want to set up a display in your store in a spot where the most customers will see it and spend the most time looking it over. You may recall from Chapter 4 that shoppers don't linger in a store's doorway. Most will wander to the right or left, in accordance with which side of the road they drive on, and linger longest over displays where there's less chance of being brushed or bumped by other shoppers.

What might interest you is *how* we know.

Simple. Someone watched.

In this case, the watching was done by a respected research company by the name of Envirosell, led by Paco Underhill. Envirosell does smart research: They hide researchers and cameras in real stores and secretly *watch* what real customers do. This is how they have learned which direction most shoppers turn upon entering a store, and that customers linger longer at display tables where they're less likely to collide with other shoppers.

Better still, Envirosell has documented that this kind of behavior is *consistent*. If most people in the United States turn right upon entering a sufficient representation of stores under study, chances are most people will also turn right upon entering yours. So for maximum exposure, you can plop your display to the customer's right with confidence, surrounded by a buffer zone to minimize collisions.

In the preceding chapter, I described the part that color plays in the attraction and holding power of casino slot machines. The gaming industry didn't learn to use color by interviewing slot players. They tried different colors. And watched and counted.

STORE OR NO STORE, NO PROBLEM

It's remarkably simple when you think about it.

To learn whether to package your product in green or pink, don't ask yourself what you would prefer, and skip the focus groups. Instead, make a reasonable quantity in both colors. Put green in some stores and pink in others. Then, after a few days, count. Then switch the stores and the colors, wait a few more days, and count again. Repeat the trial to rule out flukes, and count again. In short order, you'll know which color, if either, people prefer.

If you don't have access to stores, create two flyers offering a free trial size of the product. Show a photo of the product in a green package on half of the flyers and in a pink one in the other half. Write the copy so that people must call, mail, or go online to request the product, using a free offer code that, unbeknownst to them, corresponds to the package color, or provide a unique return address, phone number, or URL for each color. Collate the flyers so that every other one is green or pink, and have them inserted in a newspaper. Then, count your orders by the code, address, phone, or URL to which people respond. Correlate the replies to the color, and in short order you'll know which one sells better. Instead of asking people to tell you which color they prefer, you're letting them *show* you, uninhibited by any knowledge of someone's watching or counting.

There are other ways to let people *show* you how they will behave.

To learn which headline appeals to more people, create two pamphlets that are identical in every way except for the headline. Now run a classified newspaper ad that has both titles but that allows people to choose only one to receive free. Count the requests. The pamphlet receiving more requests has the stronger headline. (You can also use this technique to test taglines, if you insist on having one.)

Or, find a magazine that will enclose your flyer with the publication in a poly-wrap bag or accept it as a bind-in. Print two versions of the flyer, again identical but for the headline and, in this case, the phone number. Offer something free—the same offer for each version—and deliver the flyers collated so that every other magazine ends up carrying every other version. The two versions will be distributed evenly among the publication's readers, making each group truly representative. From there, it's a simple matter of counting. The phone number that rings with the greater number of free offer requests is on the ad with the more productive headline. Test enough headlines in this way and a winning headline will emerge for you to use across the board.

To learn which direct mail offer works better, create two or more versions and send them to alternating names on your mailing list. Count the replies.

To learn which TV spot or station sells more, run two or more versions over similar schedules with different phone numbers. Count the calls.

With a little imagination, you can learn for yourself how people react to just about anything—down to details like borders and background colors—just by watching and counting.

Flukes happen, so it's always a good idea to repeat any test. Once you have a successful test, it's also a good idea to continue discrete tests of new approaches against it. You never know when a new tactic will prove itself more effective than the established winner.

ONLINE TESTING ON THE FLY

The Internet provides an accelerated tool for this kind of comparative testing called *Web optimization.*

A web site can automatically reorganize its features so that every person who logs on sees a different combination of colors, prices, layouts, appeals, headlines, copy, and so on. Because the site also tracks sales, it's possible over time to learn which features and *combinations* of features sell best.

MULTIVARIATE TESTING

Testing as I've described it so far requires time and patience. When you test Approach A against Approach B, you must await results before choosing a winner to test against Approach C. If you're on a shorter timeframe, have a little leeway on your budget, and have a good analyst working for you, you can speed things up with *multivariate testing*.

Multivariate testing lets you mix, match, test, and evaluate multiple combinations of tactics, all at the same time.

Using specialized software that runs hundreds of algorithms and statistical arrays, a data analyst can measure the impact of each tactic over multiple combinations. You can evaluate each tactic against its "counter-tactic," plus its relative impact within each combination. In short order, you can determine the most effective combination of creative approaches, elements, incentives, and other features.

A major advantage of multivariate testing is speed. If you're using direct mail, you can learn in a few weeks what might otherwise take a year or more of testing. On the Web, you can learn as much in days or, in some cases, even hours.

Though a multivariate test may require a slightly larger up-front investment, it can be less costly than a year or more of repeated A/B tests, since you needn't test to huge markets. In fact, you can attain reliable results by targeting the same overall sample size you would need to run a viable A/B test.

Analyzing multivariate test data is tricky. The more *variables* and *strategies* you build into your test, the trickier the analysis gets. There are strict rules and intricacies to master. Multivariate testing is not for beginners.

THREE REAL-WORLD MINI-CASES

One of our clients wanted to know which of four advertising appeals would work best. Using the client's own newsletter as a test vehicle, we created four different versions of the back page. Each version displayed a different ad and referred readers to a unique landing page on the Web. When we tallied results, a clear winner emerged, pulling three times the number of Web hits as the others combined. One of the ads pulled nothing at all! Choosing which ads to retire and which to retain was an easy decision from there.

To generate qualified leads for a company that sells natural gas fireplaces, we devised three different TV spots—each with its own phone number—and ran all three for a week. By the end of the week, the winning spot outpulled the second-place spot two to one, and the third-place spot twenty to one. The client was left with no doubt as to which spot to back with the rest of the budget.[4]

A financial client hired us to sell consumer loans through direct mail. For an initial test, we took two small samples from a random selection of their mailing list and sent each a vastly different approach. One approach outsold the other three to one. This simple test effectively increased our client's Return on Advertising Investment 300 percent when we rolled out the winning version to the remainder of the list.[5]

Every direct marketer knows there is a particular order to what to test in a campaign. First, test to be sure you are reaching the right market. The most brilliant creative work is powerless when it lands in front of the wrong people, while refining your targeting can produce dramatic sales increases.[6] Second, test to be sure you are offering the right incentive to encourage immediate response. We *doubled* telephone responses for the natural gas fireplace campaign by adding to our TV spot a free offer for a $1.00 jar of honey. Tellingly, the above-referenced test ad that pulled no reply at all was the only one of the four that omitted a free incentive offer. People need a reason to "act now." A freebie for those who do is a powerful tool. Last, begin testing various creative elements.

OTHER INSIGHTS FROM TESTING

The ability to pinpoint headlines, layouts, and appeals that perform best is plenty of reason to conduct predictive tests.

But marketers committed to testing for the long haul can learn a good deal more.

For a national client that provides an in-home cleaning service, we went beyond testing creative approaches and watched buyer demographics, the time of year people bought, local weather conditions at the time of purchase, and the interval between major home improvements and the time of purchase. The last element provided a useful, surprising insight: after a specific kind of home improvement purchase, customers were significantly more likely to buy our client's service within the first month, much less likely to buy in months 2 through 17, and more likely to resume purchasing again in months 18 through 24. By overlaying these and other observations about customer purchasing habits gathered over time, we increased response by 33 percent—*without* increasing the marketing expenditures.

TESTING ON A SHOESTRING

Sometimes advertising budgets don't allow for the scale of testing I've described so far. That's okay. With a little imagination, you can come up with smaller-scale, less costly ways to test, and still end up with equally valid, projectable results.

A little-known musical artist of my acquaintance was producing a CD. He knew that the cover design could make or kill a sale at point of purchase, but he didn't have the budget to produce and test multiple versions. So he bought some empty jewel cases, designed a selection of covers, printed them using a color laser printer, duplicated the CD on a home system, and thus hand-assembled these rudimentary samples at negligible cost. Stacking the competing CDs side by side on a tray, he stopped people at random and said, "We're giving away prerelease sample CDs of a new artist. The covers are different, but the CD inside is the same. Please take one, free." Every time someone took a CD, he replaced it so that the stacks remained equal in height, and he regularly switched the stacks to compensate for people who might favor the right or left. In no time, he saw that people consistently chose one cover design and ignored the others. This is how he chose the final cover design when he moved into the mass production phase.

A health plan client lacked significant funds for testing, yet wanted to test for the strongest promotional booklet cover. We dummied three booklets, each with a different cover, stopped people in a mall at random, told them our company offered three different health plans, and invited them to look them over. We switched the order of the stacks to compensate for right-middle-left biases, and paid strict attention to which brochures people picked up first and spent the most time examining. Within two hours, we knew which cover had the strongest visual appeal.

In both the CD and brochure tests, test subjects were not told that a test was afoot, nor were they asked to choose the version they preferred. In the first test, they were told to take a CD. In the second, they were told to examine the brochures. The researchers simply watched.

If time or budget absolutely will not permit testing, I have two suggestions. One, consider which one you can better afford—to spend a bit more than you'd hoped in testing, or to blow your entire budget on your best guess with no room for failure. Two, if you *must* proceed without testing, get to know what direct marketers have already tested—and use what they've learned. Join the Direct Marketing Association, read publications like *What's Working*, *DM News*, and *Direct*, and make yourself familiar with books like *Direct Marketing Rules of Thumb: 1,000 Practical and Profitable Ideas to Help You Improve Response, Save Money, and Increase Efficiency in Your Direct Program* by Nat G. Bodian.[7]

RULES OF THE GAME

There are right and wrong ways to conduct tests. Since the idea is to come up with a reliable predictor of what will succeed, we'd better go over them.

Test in the real world. Do not ask people which ad they think they'd respond to or what product they think they'd buy. Do not ask them to imagine or evaluate. In fact, don't ask people to think. Instead, make them *act*—without knowing you're watching. They mustn't know they're part of a test or that anyone is watching.

Sometimes you won't be able to test without its being obvious that you're doing research. In such cases, the trick is to avoid revealing what you're really looking for. Note that when we showed people CD covers and health care booklets, we didn't ask them which one they *liked* or *thought* they'd be likely to buy. We simply invited people to take a CD and *watched* which one they chose. We simply invited people to examine a health plan and *watched* which one they chose.

Isolate variables. Unless you're doing multivariate testing, pitting two fully divergent approaches against one another will reveal which sells more, but it won't tell you why. Did a test ad work better because the headline was stronger, because the photo was more appealing, because the font was easier to read, or because of the synergy of all three elements?

If you're testing headlines (for example), be sure the *only* difference between ads *A* and *B* is the headline. I flubbed this one myself once when I was testing two marketing approaches for the same product. One approach used a straight pitch; the other used a story.

Unfortunately, I also changed how the required legal language was presented in the story version. When one version seriously outsold the other, we knew which to roll out, but we didn't know whether it was the approach, the presentation of the legalese, or both that made the difference.

If you want to test two different headlines and two different photos at the same time, you can, but that means you'll have four versions to keep track of separately. Three variables of each means you'll have nine, and four means you'll have sixteen. Each time you introduce a variable, you must set up your test so that you can isolate its effects in the post-analysis stage. With enough support, volume, and good tracking, you can test as many distinct combinations as you wish.

Keep testing. When a winning approach surfaces, make it your control, but keep inventing and testing new approaches with small samples of your customers. You might just come up with a new, bigger winner. For a large industrial forms printer, we found a strategy that performed well, but we kept testing new ones against it just in case. Two years later, a new tactic outsold the heretofore established winner two-to-one. It became the new standard, doubling our client's sales without increasing marketing expenditures.

Here's another reason to keep testing: Sometimes a winning approach wears out. When that happens, you'll be glad if you have a new, fresher one ready to take over.

Keep and roll out the winners. Perhaps you received a subscription offer from the *Wall Street Journal* that tells of "two young men" with similar backgrounds, one of whom turns out to be far more financially successful than the other. The *WSJ* used this direct mail package to build subscriptions for decades. Estimates are that this direct mail package is accountable for over two billion dollars in *WSJ* subscriptions.

Not all marketers are as smart as the folks at the *Wall Street Journal*. Believe it or not, many *stop* after a successful test. I've heard some interesting reasons: "We're out of budget," "It's not in the plan," "We're going to try something fresh." A successful test means you'll make money if you roll it out to the rest of your market, and a successful rollout means *you should roll it out again!* When you're succeeding is not the time to stop.

Accept the outcome of tests. It's not easy being human. We like to be right. But when test results contradict your gut intuition, tell your gut to get over it.

When a test conclusively showed that our client's favored offer was ineffective, he leaned back in his chair and said, "The test is wrong. I know what my customers want." By mistaking his personal appraisal of what mattered to his customers, he ended up unwittingly clinging to an ineffective strategy.

Another client rejected a proposal backed by documentation showing that the recommended technique consistently produced sizable profits for one company after another, saying, "I just don't believe this kind of thing works."

Fortunately, not all marketing decision makers are myopic. When we created a major prospecting campaign for a bank, the CEO was skeptical but allowed us to test it anyway. When positive results rolled in, he said, "I wouldn't believe it if I hadn't seen the numbers myself. I still don't like the campaign. Now please keep it going." On another occasion, an advertising manager called me into his office to complain about an ad layout and order it replaced with another version. I happened to have fresh results for the ad in my pocket. It had outsold the other version with the more appealing layout seven-to-one. "Keep running it," he growled.

Be willing to admit defeat. Not every test produces a winner, and not every product will fly. If test after test fails to produce a winner, perhaps no one wants your product. Be glad you found out by using small tests instead of by investing in a costly, unsuccessful marketing campaign.

Cutting bait isn't easy to do, especially if you happen to be an ad agency recommending that a client end your program, or you're an employee who championed the test. I have recommended cutting bait to clients myself at the risk of losing agency billings.[8]

Test small, but not too small. I recently visited with a company cheering about their "ten percent response." Then I learned they'd had one purchase after sending a direct mail package to a whopping 10 people. Oops. Ten people do not a valid sample make.

I knew a manager who boasted, "Every time I've gone on a sales call, I've returned with the order." He used this information to chastise sales people who had more total sales but closed fewer than 100 percent of prospects. I later learned that he made a total of three sales calls in five years on the job, and had cherry-picked the most likely prospects to visit. Hardly valid from a statistical standpoint.

Too few failures can mean you're uncommonly skilled or uncommonly lucky, and too few successes can mean the opposite. But it can also mean you're not testing a large enough sample. Samples needn't be huge, but it's important to make them large enough for statistical significance. As a general rule, you should have at least 30 replies before you start drawing conclusions. For more reliable conclusions, you may wish to apply any of a number of online significance factor calculators for help.

Don't move the target. If you're selling a product to senior citizens with insomnia, be sure your test reaches senior citizens with insomnia. Once you have a successful test, be sure to roll it out to senior citizens with insomnia.

Retest. Flukes happen. Before you bet the farm on a surprising test outcome, play scientist: scrutinize your methods, consider alternative explanations, and retest to be sure.

KEEP THE WINNERS . . . AND KEEP GOING

Every agency has at least one tale of a client who complains of being tired of the current campaign, only to learn that the campaign, still in the design stage, has yet to go public. So imagine how tired one might grow of a campaign that's been in the media for months or even years.

Resist the temptation to change for change's sake. Once you have a winner, keep using it and tracking its performance. As long as it produces profits, never mind how weary of it you become. Most marketing objectives do not include, "To continue providing entertainment to the people doing the marketing."

PREDICTING THE WINNERS

There is a right and a wrong way to predict customer behavior. I shall invite you to accompany me to the office restroom for a final illustration. But first, circulate a survey asking people if they wash before leaving said facilities. Make sure they know they're answering with complete anonymity, or 100 percent will answer in the affirmative.

Okay, time to visit the restroom. Choose a stall from which you can tell, without recognizing individuals, when people wash. Hang an "out of order" sign on the outside and then hide inside with the door closed. Now, count. (Tip: Don't get caught hiding in there. It will be hard to explain, and I won't back up your story.)

If your results are typical, between 60 and 80 percent of your survey respondents will say they wash, but only about 10 to 20 percent actually do when they think no one is watching.[9]

Even in anonymous surveys, asking people to explain or predict their behavior is pointless. Some people lie, but more often they simply haven't a clue about what they do or would do, much less why they'd do it.

The wrong way to predict the success of a marketing campaign is to ask people how they think they'll react to it. The right way is to find the marketer's equivalent of a restroom stall, hide inside, and take notes.

If the testing methodology presented in this chapter strikes you as disarmingly simple, I would agree. Don't let its apparent simplicity fool you. By testing marketing tactics in a real-world setting, with real people who are unaware that a test is afoot or that anyone is watching, you will learn what works, what works better, and what doesn't work at all.

There simply is no reason to bet your marketing budget on a campaign that hasn't been proven on a valid test basis.

If you want to ask people what they think of your marketing, by all means go ahead and ask. You may pick up gems of insight and be glad you asked. But do not mistake their feedback for a valid prediction of how they will react to your marketing.

The late John Wanamaker famously lamented, "I know that half of what I spend on advertising is wasted; I only wish I knew which half." Good news, marketers. With a little imagination and restraint, and without spending a bundle, you can prune the losers and identify the winners early. Which means, if you're smart, you can avoid wasting that elusive half in the first place.

SUMMARY POINTS FROM
HOW TO PREDICT A MARKET SUCCESS

- When most people react repeatedly to the same situation in the same way, we can predict with a high degree of reliability that most people will continue reacting to the same situation in exactly the same way.

- When people know they're being observed or a test is afoot, their behavior changes.

- It's important to devise tests that let people behave in what, *from their point of view*, is the real world.

- If need be and with a little imagination, you can conduct valid tests on a shoestring.

- If you *must* reveal that you're gathering research, be sure to hide what you're really trying to find out.

- Small tests keep failures small. Statistically valid small successes can indicate big wins ahead.

- Roll out winners. A test that consistently succeeds on a small scale usually succeeds on a large one.

- Isolate variables when testing.

- Flukes happen. It's always a good idea to validate results by retesting.

- Never retire a winning campaign simply because you're tired of it.

- Once you find a winner, keep running small tests against it. You never know when a new winner might emerge to replace the old one.

10

THE SCIENCES CAST A LIGHT ON MARKETING

So far we've focused on the benefits of approaching marketing like a scientist. But there's also value in approaching *science* like a *marketer*.

The cognitive sciences reveal a good deal about the origins and motivators of human behavior. We can only hope that someday these findings will help us better deal with social problems, crime, even war. In the meantime, a look at what drives our behavior can help marketers adopt brand values with intrinsic human appeal. It's not an altogether insignificant application of science. Good marketing has been known to speed improvements in quality of life. Insights that help marketers better serve customers—who happen to be people—have value, regardless of whatever higher purposes those insights may have the potential to fill.

What you're about to read is likely to challenge some of your assumptions about humankind or even yourself. You may be tempted to dismiss this information as psychobabble. I assure you it is not. Like any science, psychology and evolutionary psychology began as speculation. Though their histories are rife with quacks and quackery, they are well-supported fields today. Despite much that remains to be discovered, marketers ignore the science of what we now know about ourselves at their own peril.

PREWIRED BEHAVIOR

The emerging science of evolutionary psychology, a branch of sociobiology and ethology, indicates that behavioral traits are as evolved and heritable as physical traits.[1] Indeed, they evolve together. The ability to spray noxious fluid is useless to the skunk that fails to evolve a turn-and-fire instinct. The ability to decorate a nest is useless to the bowerbird unless the male evolves the decorating instinct *and* the female evolves the instinct of responding. Echolocation is useless to the bat or dolphin that fails to develop the instinct to use it for sight.

A good deal of *human* behavior appears to be just as instinctive. While some of our behaviors are learned[2] and some are shaped by our social environment,[3] many of our behaviors appear prewired and do not require learning or the influence of society to bring them out.[4]

Once we accept that human behavior can be instinctive and heritable, much of our behavior in the marketplace begins to make sense in new ways.

BACK TO THE HABITAT

It may be a puzzle why moths fly to their doom the moment you light a fire, or why some dogs urinate when they greet you at the door and only increase production when you shout *No!*

The mysteries unravel when you consider that moths and canines haven't frequented human homes for long. Moths rely on light from celestial bodies to navigate. They have not adapted to man-made light sources like candles, fireplaces, and electric lights, all of which only throw off their natural navigation system. Wild canines[5] fall on their backs and urinate to show submission to a dominant pack member. Peeing at your feet is a show of deference, and yelling at the poor dog only incites it to increase the show.[6]

Likewise, if you want to understand human behavior, you'll need to take a look at how a given behavior may have served us in our original habitat. We didn't evolve in cities of concrete and glass, in cars hurtling down freeways at 75-plus miles per hour, nor sitting at desks for hours on end barking orders at subordinates.[7] Our original environment was Africa, where we lived a nomadic existence with minimal or no clothing under a blazing sun, gathering naturally occurring produce and, when we were in the mood for a good steak, hunting game.

But we changed our environment fast—blindingly fast, in geological terms. Leaving equatorial zones and heading north allowed and perhaps forced humans to cultivate crops and raise game,[8] which led to trading our natural nomadic existence and small groups for year-round settlements and larger communities. Advances in cultivation allowed one person to produce food for many, in time freeing others to specialize as caretakers, builders, hunters, cooks, artists, and priests. Trade inevitably arose, and rudimentary economies were born.

Though humankind took only a few millennia to change its environment from nomadic to agricultural, and only

about the last century to overhaul it from agricultural to industrial to technological, true evolution in slow-reproduc-
ing creatures like humans takes longer.[9] This includes
psychological change. That's why most civilized adult men
who have learned to avoid killing a rival during courtship
still experience an underlying desire to do the rival bodily
harm. This may appear a baffling and superfluous compulsion in today's world of romance with roses, chocolates,
and serenades. But consider how gorillas, elk, and wolves
compete—and humans once competed—for mates in the
wild, and a lingering desire to beat up the nearest contend-
er begins to make sense. (And, we hope, it remains
repressed.[10])

So to understand *what people do* in the marketplace, simply observe them (see Chapter 6). To understand *why they
do it*, look for how that behavior may have served us in a
prehistoric hunter-gatherer existence.

By definition, there is no written record of prehistory—
which covers most of our existence as a species—and you
and I weren't around to see it firsthand. But we have reliable sources of information about life in those days. We can
learn a lot by studying other social creatures like apes,
wolves, dolphins, even vampire bats. We can learn by
studying the few primitive human populations still around
today. And we can learn a good deal from clues left in our
own DNA.[11]

As we sort through the data, we begin to see that much
of our behavior in the marketplace likely evolved to serve
us in a primitive setting and followed us into our modern
world. Here, it continues to find expression, sometimes
continuing to serve us well, sometimes not, but often fooling us when it comes to understanding what truly motivates us.

Take automobile ownership. A car is a requirement for living in most modern cities. But an understanding of evolutionary psychology can cast light upon our desire for a *shiny, new* car. That desire, it turns out, may be as innate as our compulsion to walk upright.

Let's have a look at this and other selected examples of how the psychology we evolved millennia ago continues to influence our behavior in today's marketplace. At the same time, we'll examine how marketers can use this understanding to deliver better brand values to customers. We may just stumble upon insights your gut would never have imagined.

WHEN SEX SELLS, WHEN IT DOESN'T, AND WHY

Every so often some fool—usually male, I'm loathe to admit—thinks he can sell products to men by putting a half-clad woman in an advertisement. The alleged gut-based rationale: Sex sells.

Clearly sex sells *itself*, as evidenced by thriving porn and sex toy industries. But let's set those aside while we explore whether sex sells other kinds of products.

You won't learn how gender and sex figure into purchase decisions from focus groups, but you'll learn a good deal if you interview a few peacocks and peahens. Consider how the peacock attracts the peahen: He displays that amazing tail. The fellow with the most impressive tail feathers wins the most hens.

While there is some argument for sexual selection by flight of fancy—maybe the first peahens to favor ostentatious tail displays were moved by nothing more substantive than what moves humans to embrace the fashion *du jour*—the evidence favors an unconscious quest on the part of females to secure prime genetic material for future offspring. A peacock must divert considerable resources from the normal business of maintaining a healthy body to grow and display something as frivolous and ornamental as those amazing tail feathers. Those who do clearly have strength to spare. Thus, peahens that happen to be attracted to males with surplus strength stand a better chance of ending up with stronger chicks, which in turn stand a better chance of surviving to reproduce.

This has a compounding effect. Males resort to an ostentatious show of genetic wealth to compete for female attention, while females wax selective about males. The offspring of strong males and picky females tend to be healthier than peers, so they out-compete them in mating, thus preserving genes linked to large displays of tail feathers in males and genes linked to a preference for them in females. Their descendants, in time, dominate the species. Thus, the survival game—that of getting one's genes into the next generation—inevitably goes to the strongest males and the pickiest females. And just who are the strongest males? The ones with the sexiest tail feathers. So when a peahen is near, a peacock competes with rivals by spreading those feathers—even though *why* is doubtless utterly lost on him.

Nature has many like examples. Male mallard ducks and pheasants are famously ornamented, while the females are famously plain. Male bowerbirds prove they have resources to spare by spending time and energy collecting trinkets to ornament their nests, and other male birds show strength by trying to out-sing one another. Male lions and gorillas sport their virility by sprouting manes, moose by growing antlers (and employing them in the dispatch of rivals), and wolves by simply growing larger with bigger teeth.

Now consider the male human. Acknowledging that there are unusually short men and unusually tall women, *on average*, men tend to be larger and stronger, and ornamented with body and facial hair. Women seem attracted to a man's height, hairy chest, broad shoulders, and dark eyelashes. Perhaps evolution helped shape a male human who wins female attention by showing off his excess resources with a shameless display of stature and body hair.

Though most men today shave the facial hair and hide the body hair under clothing (or, increasingly, shave it off), our modern age provides *other* means for men to display surplus assets. Like bowerbirds that decorate their nests, human males decorate themselves with newer and bigger cars, expensive clothes, expensive fragrances, and expensive toys.

Meanwhile, because humans tend to be monogamous (or nearly so), the fittest women have an incentive to compete for the fittest men. Thus the importance of fashion, cosmetics, and even cosmetic surgery for women.[12]

So when it comes to the role of sex in selling, it's important to note that in nature *males compete with males and females compete with females.* That is why people spend to excess on outer appearances like expensive cars and clothing: it's all about outcompeting members of one's own sex.

So the next time a flight of fancy tells you to put a sexy woman in an ad selling a men's product, or vice versa, ignore it. Neither sex will be impressed with your product if you merely adorn it with attractive, minimally clad representatives of the opposite sex. To sell wrenches to men, include a photo of a credible man using your wrenches; to sell them to women, include a photo of a credible woman using them. If you include a photo of a Victoria's Secret model using your wrenches, you will attract attention from both sexes, but the wrenches will go unnoticed.

Direct marketing experience backs this up. Direct response radio spots with female announcers sell better to women; male announcers sell better to men. Direct response mail and print ads fare better when they feature photos of men using products for men and of women using products for women.

THE MORAL BRAND

At first glance, "survival of the fittest" might seem to connote "every one for oneself." In many species, this is the case. Bacteria, viruses, plants, frogs, fish, and snakes are not famous for nurturing their young or for setting aside self-interest to benefit the clan. From birth, these creatures are responsible for procuring their own food and for saving their own skin from predators. From their proliferation, we must concede that "every one for oneself" is a sound strategy for many species' survival and growth.

But "all for one and one for all" is also a successful strategy. Creatures who happen to put the group's interest ahead help ensure the long-term survival of the group—despite the occasional immediate risk to the individual.

Take, for instance, vampire bats. After a hunt, vampire bats return home and regurgitate their spoils for group consumption. This more or less evens out the take among the day's most and least successful hunters. But woe unto the occasional bat that hoards its own take. When these selfish bats inevitably experience bad hunts of their own, fellow bats remember their bad behavior and exclude them from sharing. Even vampire bats, it seems, display a sense of justice.

You would be right to call the sharing and punishment behavior of vampire bats a primitive version of "You scratch my back, I'll scratch yours; if you don't scratch my back, I'll be damned if I'll scratch yours." If you were an evolutionary psychologist, you would call this behavior "reciprocal altruism."[13]

Reciprocal altruism isn't unique to vampire bats. Dolphins unite against sharks. Wolves have rules for hunting, feeding, and mating that promote the overall welfare of the pack. Chimpanzees practice politics that are disturbingly similar to those of humans, including siding with winners, comforting losers, using sex as a bargaining chip, and throwing tantrums to attract attention or sympathy or get their way. Even ants and bees have group rules.

Reciprocal altruism in nature isn't merely learned. It is as hardwired into bats, dolphins, wolves, chimps, ants, and bees as echolocation, surfacing for air, marking territory, climbing trees, farming aphids, and making honey.

What should be significant to marketers is that a sense of reciprocal altruism—a basic understanding of how we relate to and treat one another—comes as naturally to most of us as talking with our hands.[14]

When a marketer is willing to scratch a shopper's back, shoppers find themselves more inclined to scratch in return by trusting the marketer, and by repeatedly returning to spend more. When Nordstrom gives you a no-hassle refund because your outfit just doesn't seem right, you reward them with increased loyalty and purchasing. When Time-Life lets you examine a book with no obligation and includes a gift you can keep even if you return the book, you're more likely to entrust them with your credit card number. When after a few poisonings Tylenol goes to extremes to pull product from shelves, even though statistically most of the product is certainly safe, we are inclined to trust them when they restock later.

Marketers who want to be around for the long haul do well to practice reciprocal altruism. Treating customers morally and ethically, even on occasion giving them the benefit of the doubt, is good business precisely because it resonates with evolved humanity.

For many early marketers, this notion seemed counterintuitive and risky. What was to keep people from returning perfectly good products and simply *claiming* dissatisfaction? Happily, experience has shown trustworthiness to be an inherent trait present in the majority of humans, most of the time.

There are, of course, limits and abuses. On both sides.

BRANDS THAT CHEAT

A subordinate wolf knows not to make attempts on the dominant wolf's mate or dinner. The penalties can be painful, as people who have suffered even the smallest dog bite can attest. But should Dominant Wolf abandon a meal, even for a moment, Subordinate Wolf might, after a quick assessment finding the odds of being caught minimal, steal a morsel, if not the whole thing.

This should sound eerily human to you. Along with the ability to consider the welfare of the group, we have also inherited the ability to willfully bend the rules. Each of us determines our own boundaries of what we consider permissible. Some of us, upon finding a spider in the house, escort it safely outside; others, shoe in hand, maniacally pound it into oblivion.

For most creatures, including humans, the suitability of bending a rule is often governed by the twin universal standards, "What are my odds of getting caught?" and "If I'm caught, how serious will the consequences be?"[15]

Companies are no different. When risk and consequences appear minimal, some set aside ethics and proceed. Consider unethical practices within the mortgage loan industry . . . "New Age" companies that sell worthless health products with outlandish promises . . . banks that issue low-rate credit cards carefully designed to manipulate even astute customers into penalties and high default rates . . . so-called psychics who relieve innocent believers of big dollars in exchange for telling them their deceased loved ones are doing well . . . network marketing schemes that promise instant riches without work . . . the list goes on.

It's unreasonable to expect a wolf to pause before pilfering a meal to consider whether pilferage is the right thing to do. But it's not unreasonable to expect it of people. People have the unique ability to overrule natural impulses for the greater good. They also have the ability to do the opposite, but with proper controls—like supervision, surveillance, and big-picture understanding—most resist the temptation.

When building brand values, marketers decide what kind of creature their organization will be. Will it take ruthless advantage of or stick up for its customers? Both strategies have proven viable in regard to profitability. We might speculate that companies with ethical practices are more likely to prosper over the long haul, but such speculation would do little to persuade people concerned only with short-term profits.

Fortunately, customers are not left entirely at the mercy of unethical marketers. They can and do vote with their wallets. They can and do enact laws.

And, they have gossip.

GOSSIP CAN BE A GOOD THING

Vampire bats can detect and punish only the cheaters they catch firsthand. Humans have a unique tool that enhances a cheater's odds of getting caught: unlike bats, humans can gossip. You needn't catch a cheater in the act to withdraw your trust. All you need is to hear it from someone who heard it from someone else who allegedly saw it happen.

Gossip can have serious implications for the would-be long-term marketer. When Ford opted to pay for lawsuits rather than engineer away the Pinto's tendency to explode on impact, word spread and humans with long memories punished the automaker for years. Today with the Internet, viral communication spreads reports of infractions market-wide in a matter of hours. When Wal-Mart was accused of violations against employees, an incensed nation knew about it right away. A home video of rats overrunning a Taco Bell in New York City went viral within a day. Web sites dedicated to revealing unsavory credit card practices gain hits daily.

Marketers not only provide products and services; they also build *reputations*. Marketers who persist in disappointing customers risk eventual loss at the cash register. Gossip as a useful aspect for group order appears to be more than a cultural phenomenon. It seems to be an evolved trait that we have extended into the marketplace. And if it keeps more marketers on their toes, so much the better.

CUSTOMERS WHO CHEAT

Cheating isn't the exclusive domain of marketers. Customers cheat too. I warn every new mail-order client that free incentives and money-back guarantees are necessary tools of the trade, but to expect abuses. Some consumers falsely claim not to have received the product. Others will order to obtain the incentive gift with no intention of purchasing the product. Retailers with generous return policies must endure people who wear out products and return them as "defective" and demand replacements. Or, worse, who attempt to return products the retailer never in fact carried. At the extreme, there are those who slip a mouse into a Pepsi can or a severed finger into a serving of Wendy's chili and then file a lawsuit.

On the bright side, these infractions are in the minority. When they occur, the general public expresses outrage at the would-be scammer rather than at the targeted marketer. Otherwise, goodwill in business would cease as a viable strategy.

SALESPERSON AS PREDATOR

Wolves, bats, lions, eagles, crocodiles, and the like are clear-cut predators. We humans have confused things for ourselves.

In our original wild state, we were clear-cut predators too. We hunted game and hunted produce. When we started keeping herds and planting crops, we changed the rules governing our behavior. Suddenly not every resource was fair game: now there were ownership rights to be respected. But natural selection hasn't had time to change our psychology. The predator within, whose behavior is largely deemed wrong by today's standards, is still very much alive and still finds expression.

We use the word *criminal* for people who surrender their will to the inner predator to the extreme. Fortunately, most people learn to compete within the rules society sets.

The classic rainmaker is often someone who has learned to use the inner predator in a business setting. This person loves to hunt new business but, once securing it, grows bored and, eager to engage in another hunt, hands the spoils off to the cooks.

Many successful salespeople are ethical, but not all. Most sales training programs teach selling as the process of identifying and filling needs. Sadly, not all salespeople stop there. Some exploit the slightest weakness and stretch the truth for the sake of the sale. Ethical salespeople balance the inner predator with a finely tuned sense of reciprocal altruism.

PATTERN SEEKING AND THE BRAND

Humans are a pattern-seeking species. Survival in the wild depended on our ability to recognize and capitalize on consistency. Knowing that a certain leaf shape signaled edible vegetation, that dark clouds signaled a need to take cover, and that a shaking rattle signaled a not-very-suitable plaything had much to do with our sticking around long enough to reproduce.

Smart marketers capitalize on the human affinity for consistency. It is good branding practice for all McDonald's restaurants to sport the same colors and menu, for all Mercedes-Benz cars to feature superb engineering, for all Macintosh peripherals to plug in and work, and for all health care professionals to wear scrubs. The practice succeeds because humans are programmed to recognize and depend on consistency.

AUTHORITY AND THE BRAND

Part of human survival in the wilderness can be credited to our ability to rely on the sage advice of our elders. Human children don't have to learn firsthand the inadvisability of stepping on cacti or the danger of approaching a mountain lion. At an early age, we learn to accept and profit from the advice of authority figures without subjecting their claims to scrutiny.

Marketers capitalize on our respect for authority in a number of ways. They dress representatives in crisp uniforms or tasteful suits. They hire radio announcers with deep, reassuring voices. They tout their years of experience. They publish testimonials. They use celebrity endorsements (sometimes with success, sometimes not). They quote favorable reviews. They even *invent* characters we learn to trust.[16]

INNER SECURITY AND BRAND RECOGNITION

During the 1960s in the United States, it became fashionable to believe that humankind is peaceful by nature. Crime, war, and other acts of violence were interpreted as symptoms of a broken society. Anthropologist Margaret Mead did much to promote the notion of a "gentle savage" with her studies of New Guinean and Samoan native peoples, whom she alleged were peaceful and harmless by nature. What she failed to account for is another human trait as innate as our ability to do violence: that of putting our best foot forward when others are watching.

Unsavory as the thought may be, there is ample evidence that to raid, war, rape, kill, and steal are all part of basic human nature.[17] But they do not reign unchecked, they are not manifest all of the time, and we do not wield them upon everyone in our path. Humans evolved to be reciprocally altruistic animals within their own clan. While out-and-out acts of violence within a clan occurred, acts of violence on competing groups were more common and acceptable. It became important for humans to learn to recognize familiar places and faces as young as possible. Infants who learned to cry at the sight of unknown faces could save their own skins and those of fellow tribe members.

Thus, trust and knowing whom to trust evolved as early human survival tools.

This matters if you want to win customers who will remain loyal to your brand. You must begin by recognizing that at some level your customers are inclined to not trust you, because they don't know you. You must earn your way into their clan. You do this by proving your trustworthiness and usefulness consistently and over time: reliable performance, real benefits, clear advantages, minimal hot air, fair policies, consistent treatment, and a familiar and inviting voice and look.

Brands that have been around a long time have an advantage in the familiarity and trust department. If you grew up eating Cracker Barrel cheese, washing your clothes with Tide, and filling your gas tank at a Chevron station, you grew up with these brands as part of your clan.

Some brands, like Harley-Davidson, Macintosh, and Steinway become clans in their own right that consumers proudly join and defend. Try telling a Harley rider that a Kawasaki motorcycle is a worthy substitute, a Mac user that PCs are as good or better, or a Steinway pianist that the instrument of the immortals might just as well be a Yamaha, and you'll end up with something of the magnitude of a religious debate on your hands.[18]

Once you earn the trust of your customers, a good overriding policy is *don't blow it*. People forgive errors—witness Bill Clinton's and Martha Stewart's continued popularity—but there are limits. Not even the huge accounting firm of Arthur Andersen could recover after mishandling Enron's audits. And when hotel magnate Leona Helmsley snobbishly revealed her view that taxes should only be paid by members of the general public—"little people," she called them—consumers actually cheered *for the IRS*.

THE POWER OF PLEASING DESIGN

In the 1960s, psychologist Paul Ekman studied human facial expressions. He found that smiles, frowns, puzzled looks, angry eyes, and other facial expressions mean the same to all people in all cultures and settings—even people isolated from so-called modern civilization.

For his trouble, he was shouted down as a racist by people who prefer to believe that all human interactions are learned. That's another story. For our purposes, what's important is that Ekman showed there is such a thing as images with universal meaning when it comes to humans.

This has implications for marketing design. Just as we find meaning in facial expressions—which are purely visual—we also innately react to visual elements such as logos, colors, fonts, page layouts, and interior design. We find some colors "warm" and others "cool." Some colors stimulate appetite. When people open a direct mail letter, their eyes first go to the signature at the bottom of the page and then drop to the "P.S." Restaurateurs know that diners prefer smaller spaces broken up by plants or partitions than large halls, and men like interior designs that let them sit facing the door. Online, more people click red buttons. People like to check boxes on order forms. People expect to find phone numbers and logos at the bottom of a magazine ad and often miss those placed at the top. By contrast, on a web page, people expect to find valuable contact information at the top.

So perhaps the look of a company's facilities and materials deserves more thought, attention, and analysis than merely opting for what the owners, their spouses, or even focus groups find appealing in an opinion survey.

MORALITY AND THE PSYCHOLOGY OF MARKETING

The idea of using evolutionary psychology in marketing may make some people uneasy. Permit me some reassurances.

Not even the most psychologically adept marketer can force a customer to act against his or her will. You can stop buying fast food wrapped in red and yellow the moment you set your mind to it. You can buy a beat-up used car and still feel attractive. An understanding of what drives us can help a marketer make it *easier* for us to buy. We still don't have to do it.[19]

If you *want* to buy, using knowledge of how to make buying easier for you needn't be manipulative or underhanded on the part of the marketer. On the contrary, using that knowledge can be thoughtful and courteous. Ask any man who, while waiting outside the dressing room in a women's store, appreciates adjacent chairs and a TV tuned to a sports station. Ask any woman who appreciates good lighting at the cosmetics counter. Ask any man or woman who appreciates thorough information at the home improvement center on how to use a tool.

Is it possible for marketers to use knowledge of human psychology to unsavory ends? Absolutely, as every Ponzi scheme reported in the news attests. Yet scoundrels needn't—and rarely do—study evolutionary psychology to prey upon the trusting and unwary. Like any other predator, they happen naturally upon their innate ability to identify and exploit prey. Revelations about what drives human behavior will not increase abuses, which do and will continue to happen on their own. If anything, evolutionary psychology can shed light on why people continue to fall for scams and, in time, perhaps equip more people to better protect themselves.

WITH THE SURFACE THUS SCRATCHED

Like many scientific fields, the study of human evolutionary psychology began with a thirst for knowledge. Promise of useful application followed.

A sound grasp of evolutionary psychology can lead to better diagnosis and treatment of psychological problems, better informed social work and programs, smarter ergonomic design, more effective education, increased workplace satisfaction, peaceful resolutions to conflict, and more.

As a field, evolutionary psychology is in its infancy. With the surface thus scratched, who knows what benefits await.

Meanwhile, the field gives marketers a glimmer of how and why we buy. Much of what we know runs counter to what we might assume. We might prefer to think that all behavior is learned or the product of societal influence . . . that suggestive photos of the opposite sex will sell mundane products . . . that customers can't be trusted . . . that altruism is an unsound business strategy . . . and so on. But, as always, a scientific approach can keep our gut intuition from leading us astray.

I might add that knowledge of human inclinations brings with it knowledge of our strong spots and, regrettably, our weak spots. To capitalize on human weakness in marketing (or in any other application) is immoral.

So, in addition to helping us better understand human nature in the marketplace, science also shows us where the high road lies.

As marketers and as people, may we all take it.

SUMMARY POINTS FROM
THE SCIENCES CAST A LIGHT ON MARKETING

- Looking at marketing like a scientist helps. So does looking at science like a marketer.

- Your gut would be surprised by how many human behavior traits are prewired and inherited.

- Understanding prewired human behavior can be useful to marketers.

- To understand human behavior, it's useful to consider our original habitat.

- Sex affects buying decisions, but not the way your gut might suggest.

- Within limits and rules and despite exceptions, customers tend to reciprocate when brands are generous and fair.

- Good ethics build stronger brands for the long haul.

- Gossip is a powerful weapon customers wield against brands that cheat.

- Predatory selling is the antithesis of reciprocal altruism.

- There are psychological drivers behind the effectiveness of good design, an appearance of authority, and brand consistency.

- Understanding human nature is an opportunity to improve marketing—and the ethics of marketing.

11

THE DISCIPLINE OF STRATEGY

S ometimes it's a shame that making advertising is such fun.[1]

Otherwise, it would be a lot less tempting to skip laying a solid strategic foundation before jumping straight to, "What's it going to say? What's it going to look like?"

Good strategy isn't necessary for creating really cool advertising, but it's essential for creating *successful* advertising, cool or not. Jumping to the creative stage without a sound strategy is like firing a gun without bothering to take aim. Lucky shots happen, but usually all you'll get is needless, costly holes.

But before you roll your eyes and prepare to be bored at the thought of advertising strategy, let me assure you that laying the strategic foundation is itself a creative, engrossing, even fascinating process. As you're about to see, working through a creative strategy will open your eyes to important factors you might otherwise overlook, point you to solutions that might otherwise elude you, and organize your thinking to guide the creative brainstorming to come.

A good creative strategy grows out of the answers to seven major questions. Don't let the seemingly elementary nature of the questions fool you. The trick is to challenge yourself and answer them in depth. Shall we get started?

WHO IS THE TARGET MARKET?

You might think that you shouldn't need a book to tell you to ask a fundamental question like, "Who is going to buy what I have to sell?" I'd have to agree—you shouldn't. Yet I've been surprised more than once at the number of people who spend perfectly good advertising money without bothering to ask this very question. Even more surprising is how a well-thought-out answer can spin your advertising in directions you hadn't expected.

A commercial check printer hired our agency to help them increase their sales of business checks. When we asked who buys business checks, the answer seemed obvious: owners of smaller companies and, in larger companies, accountants, bookkeepers, and controllers. Good. We had defined our target.

Or had we? After playing a little bit of "Oh yeah? Let's see," we realized that companies already doing business already have business checks. When the supply runs low, they don't go check shopping. They mail a reorder form, usually tucked near the bottom of their checks, back to the original check supplier. So advertising to people who were already in business might be an uphill battle and a waste of our client's money.

But what about people who *weren't* already in business? Well, people about to start a new business don't go check shopping, either. They go bank shopping. There, they find the desk marked New Accounts, open a business account, and order checks from whichever check printing company the new accounts person happens to present.

Whoa! Our market wasn't business owners or bookkeepers. It was the new accounts person! Rather than persuade business people to request our client's checks, we needed to persuade new accounts people to push them.

When we work with new clients, we always open with the question, "Who is your customer?" Not content with easy answers like "adults," "men," "women," or "teenagers," we'll ask follow-up questions like these:

- What age range do your customers fall in?
- What do they wear?
- What are their hobbies and interests?
- What kind of cars do they drive?
- How many children do they have?
- What time of day, day of the week, and month of the year do they tend to buy?
- What kind of work do they do?
- What do they read?
- Is the person who *buys* your product the same person who *uses* it?
- Who influences your customers' buying decisions? How much influence do these influencers wield?

As you work through these questions, be sure not to let self-fulfilling assumptions limit your opportunities. If you market cars exclusively to men, your sales records will likely show you that women don't buy cars—and you'll not just miss, but potentially alienate a viable market. Automakers fell into that trap well into the 1980s despite increasing numbers of women with their own careers and purchasing power. A few automakers finally woke up and began marketing to women, and later began designing cars with women in mind. Good thing. Studies today estimate that women account for about half of new and used car sales.[2]

Identifying your target market (or, *markets*) helps you figure out where to find your customers and thus select the media—TV, radio, outdoor, mail, Internet—best suited to help you put a message in front of them. The revelation that our check printer client's real target was new accounts clerks immediately influenced *when* and *where* we would place our advertising messages. You don't reach new accounts people with the same media you use to reach business owners and bookkeepers.

With your target market identified, you're in a position to address the next strategic question.

WHAT MATTERS TO THE TARGET MARKET?

Let's return to our check printer for a moment.

New accounts clerks and business owners care about different things. Knowing we were talking to new accounts people utterly changed our approach. We now knew we needed to appeal, for the most part, to women between the ages of 25 and 40. Most weren't career minded, but planned either to work only until realizing a goal (such as a degree or a major purchase) or to work for the long term with no plans of moving up. Some needed the money; some simply enjoyed the job.

I hope no reader bristles at the apparent sexist nature of those generalizations. They are only *apparently* sexist. There are male new accounts clerks. There are female new accounts clerks who will become president of the bank. But making a marketing decision requires that we acknowledge and deal with *most*, balanced by taking care to avoid creating or promoting undue stereotypes.

Most business owners think about checks only when it's time to order. Even then, their requirements are simple—reasonable cost, timely delivery, accurate information, good appearance, software compatibility, a company logo in the upper-left corner, and security. The new accounts person needs to be able to reassure the business owner about those things, but her real concerns fall more along the line of looking professional in front of her customer, not having to deal with customers whose checks were printed or delivered incorrectly, a hassle-free relationship with the check vendor, and being able to go home on time at day's end. Clearly, any message geared uniquely to the business owner would fall flat in front of the new accounts person. We also knew we would do far better with a message oriented around benefits to *her* over and above benefits to the *bank*. Yet the bank had ultimate say about the products it would offer, so we couldn't ignore the bank's interests.

WHAT ARE YOUR OBJECTIVES?

I was a guest in a meeting where an ad agency presented its media plan to a brand manager. Looking over the plan, the brand manager's eyes lit up. "We're going to do TV?" she asked.

"You have the budget for it," replied her account executive.

I had no authority in the meeting, but I had curiosity, and I lost no time in exercising it. "What's the campaign objective?" I asked.

They gaped at me as if I'd asked the non sequitur of the year. At length, the brand manager, said, "I don't know. Awareness, I guess." With that, off they went, bent on spending her money on TV, for no reason other than the fact that she had the money to spend.

It wasn't the only time I received a blank stare in return for asking about advertising objectives. In fact, it happens quite often. New clients have been known to say, "I just thought we ought to advertise. Isn't it *your* job to tell *us* the objectives?"

Establishing objectives is not your ad agency's job. Inferring them, clarifying them, challenging them—sure, that's our job. But it's up to you to know what you wish your advertising to accomplish.

To help get past the blank stare phase, I find a great starting point is to ask people to complete this sentence: *After being exposed to the advertising, the target market will_____.*

Be careful not to settle for easy answers. "Be more aware of our product" or "buy more of our product" are starting points at best. If awareness is your objective, how many people are aware of your product now? Exactly what kind of awareness do you want? Or, in other words, how do you wish to be perceived after the campaign? What percent increase of awareness will you consider successful? How will you measure awareness?[3] If selling more product is your objective, how much are you selling now? How much more do you wish to sell? By when? At what cost per sale? How will you measure the impact of the advertising on sales? How will you separate advertising from other factors that affect sales?

Good advertising objectives hold your feet to the fire. Like, "Increase top-of-mind awareness among target market from five to seven percent by the end of the third quarter." Or, "Increase consumer calls to our toll-free number by 25 percent within six months." Or, "Position our company such that 50 percent of people who are aware of us see us as environmentally responsible by year-end." Or, "Increase sales three percent and reduce cost-per-sale by ten dollars within twelve months." Now, *those* are real objectives with precious little wiggle room. They are specific and measurable. Either you hit them or you don't. They leave no place to hide.

I love objectives like that. Unlike the agency that sold TV to my brand manager friend for no reason other than to consume budgeted funds, justified at the last minute with the token goal, "awareness, I guess," I like knowing exactly what result our work needs to achieve.

The knowledge, in turn, also guides the next strategic decision.

(I should add that failing to hit objectives is not necessarily a mandate to fire anyone, including your ad agency. The whole purpose behind measurable objectives is to focus, try, evaluate, refocus, and retry.)

WHAT IS YOUR KEY CLAIM?

Now that we know who we're talking to, how we're going to reach them, and what we want to accomplish as a result, it's time to think about what we're going to say in hopes of accomplishing it.

Deciding what to say begins with identifying your *key claim*.

A key claim is the overriding message, expressed in its simplest terms, that is most likely to win your case, persuade your audience, and bring your objectives to pass.

It's what all other messages in your advertisement add up to.

It's the one point, above all others, you want to get across.

And I do mean *one* point. This can take discipline, for it's tempting to load on point after point with a little help from commas, conjunctions, and insecurity. Suppose you've about settled that your company's key claim is "new glasses in an hour." But then your quality control chief says, "You have to tell them we use high quality materials." And your customer service manager says, "We can't leave out the satisfaction guarantee." And your CEO says, "I think we need to include something about the fact that we're employee-owned." Your new key claim now goes something like this: "We're an employee-owned company that makes glasses out of high quality materials in an hour, satisfaction guaranteed." That's not a bad summary, but it's an awful key claim.

This is a key claim: "Heinz ketchup is thick and rich." This is *not*: "Heinz ketchup is thick and rich, contains more tomatoes per ounce, contains the best quality vinegar, is the preferred choice of gourmet restaurants, and is as good on a hot dog as it is on a hamburger."

The words used to define the key claim in your strategy may, but most likely won't, appear verbatim in your advertising. Right now, you're defining the claim. To express it in elegant terms will be the job of your advertising, later. So, don't worry about making your key claim euphonious. Worry about defining it so that it will work its hardest for you.

As you propose and evaluate key claims, remember that *what you want to say is irrelevant*. That is, it's irrelevant if you wish to succeed. Instead, think in terms of *what matters to your market.* Year after year, Zest soap's key claim was that Zest doesn't leave a soapy film on your body, expressed this way: "You're not fully clean unless you're Zestfully clean." They persisted with the claim because it was what their CEO wanted to say, despite the fact that the market found it unimportant, if not unbelievable.[4]

Don't let yourself off easy with a wimpy wannabe key claim. Claims like "We give unsurpassed service," "We're the best," "Our people are friendlier," and "proven integrity" may convince you and your board, but they'll fall on deaf ears in the market.

As you grope your way to a key claim, you may come upon a real problem if yours is a parity product, that is, it's just like everyone else's and you really don't have a distinguishing characteristic on which to build a key claim. All is not lost. Though die-hard fans hate to admit it, Coke and Pepsi are parity products. Their solutions? Coke's key claim, expressed in any number of ways, continues to be that it is the original. Pepsi's key claim, also expressed in myriad ways, is that it's the drink of the younger, more rebellious at heart. In both cases, the key claim addresses who uses the product, not product attributes.

Another solution for parity products is the *preemptive claim.* Listerine successfully hangs its hat on "kills germs on contact," even though almost *all* mouthwashes do that. So does gargling with whiskey. Some doctors argue that gargling with *water* is nearly as beneficial.

Wal-Mart notwithstanding, probably the weakest key claim at your disposal is "low price," for it creates no customer loyalty, fails to differentiate your product, builds no brand preference, risks implying low quality, and leaves you vulnerable to competitors who may undercut you. A key claim that establishes your product as superior and desirable will serve you far better than one that focuses on price. (You may certainly discuss pricing, if it makes strategic sense to do so, in your ad copy. In many cases, putting a price in your ad will increase sales. But it has no place in your key claim.)

When you believe you've nailed your key claim, test it—ruthlessly—with questions like these:

- Why that key claim?
- Can I prove it?
- Will my market believe it?
- What makes me think so?
- Why will my market care about the claim?
- How will the key claim bring about the desired behavior in my market?
- How will consistently putting forth this key claim help my advertising reach its objective?
- Does this key claim have the potential to endure?

If you can't answer these questions without rationalizing or minimizing, you may need to back up and look for a stronger key claim.

HOW WILL YOU BACK UP YOUR KEY CLAIM?

It's not enough to *assert* a claim. You're going to have to figure out how to make it believable.

Making it believable begins with having a key claim that is *true*. One of my clients, a floppy disk marketer, wanted his ads to say, "Quite frankly, our disks are the best in the world." I asked him if that was true. He assured me it was. Then I asked if he had scientific testing or consumer research to back up his claim. He indignantly replied,

"Well, *I* think our disks are the best in the world. So does my wife." I'm sure his parents thought so, too, but I told him we'd need to do better. A certain amount of puffery is fine, but empty boasts insult your market—and can have legal consequences.

Assuming your claim is true, you need to be prepared to prove it. This will be easier for some claims than others. Self-evident claims require a lot less work on the writer's part. When a home builder claims to use more floor joists than required by code, it's easy to prove. When a bicycle manufacturer claims to use only metal sprockets, it's easy to prove. When a pizza chain claims to use only real cheese, it's easy to prove. More fantastic claims require more work. When International Paper asserted that paper is stronger than people think, they proved it by building a bridge out of paper and driving a semi over it. When Pepsi wanted to convince people that their product tasted better than Coke, they videotaped live taste tests.[5] When Hyundai wanted to convince people they made quality cars, they came up with a then unheard-of 100,000-mile, 10-year warranty.

You don't necessarily have to go to such extremes to prove your key claim. Apple drives home claims about the Macintosh—intuitive, peripherals work out of the box, virus-resistant—with naught but two lovable onscreen characters who stand in front of a white background and just *talk*.

WHAT ARE YOUR OTHER CLAIMS?

If the process of identifying and proving a key claim leaves you exhausted, well, more grueling work lies ahead. In this part of the strategy, you get to list every product attribute you can think of, in any order, that might influence someone to buy your product. It's okay—in fact, encouraged—to list more than you can possibly use in an ad. The idea is to create a list of viable copy points to draw from when you finally sit down to write the ad.

In the process, it's possible you'll hit upon a claim with the potential to usurp your key claim. If that happens, so much the better.

I recommend expressing these claims as *features* and then translating them one at a time into *benefits*. This will help you carry the benefit orientation over into your copy.

If you just winced at the mention of features and benefits, I don't blame you. Countless victims of sales training seminars have been bored while a trainer droned on about the distinction between features and benefits.

Most sales trainers will tell you that people buy benefits, not features. This is true, and it's important. But to most people (including many of the trainers), the distinction remains unclear, so then they'll tell you that a feature is a product attribute, whereas a benefit is what the product does for the customer. Also true, and also not very clear. Finally, they'll offer some useless and inaccurate example like, "People don't buy quarter-inch drill bits; they buy quarter-inch holes."[6] At this point, most trainees, knowing they'll never get to break for lunch unless they feign comprehension, nod in agreement while secretly saying to themselves, "Huh?"

The trainers make it needlessly complicated. Here's a faster, easier way to discover a benefit behind a feature:

1. Write down the feature.
2. Add a comma.
3. Add the words "so you." But don't add a period, because, lastly, you're going to . . .
4. . . . finish the sentence, with your customer's priorities in mind.

Suppose you're selling a refrigerator with more usable cubic feet inside that is no bigger on the outside than others in its class. Here's how to wring a benefit out of both features: "It's the same size outside, but it's 15 percent bigger inside, *so you* can store more groceries without taking up more space in your kitchen."

Suppose you're selling a microwave cake mix that requires the consumer to add only water. "Just add water *so you* can enjoy a delicious treat in minutes, with no extra ingredients to fuss over and no mess to clean up."

Suppose you're selling a home course on dog training. "Includes step-by-step instructions *so you* can eliminate messes on the rug, put an end to destructive chewing, and amaze friends at how well your dog responds to commands."

There is no rule pertaining to how long your list of other claims should be. Let need dictate. An industrial tool will likely generate a longer list than a diet soft drink.

Once you have generated your list, it's a good idea to rank the claims. "Lasts up to three times longer than other air fresheners" will likely rank higher than "container made of domestic plastic." Odds are you won't be able to use all your claims in the finished ad. Having more benefits than you can use is a good thing. Not having enough to build a convincing case isn't.

WHAT TONE WILL YOUR CAMPAIGN TAKE?

Now that you've figured out who you're talking to, how to reach them, what matters to them, what your key claim is, how you'll prove it, and what other claims you may add, it's time to decide what kind of personality you wish to convey in your message.

Will your advertising be warm? Deadly serious? Reassuring? Tongue-in-cheek? No-nonsense? Aloof? Funny?

The tone you choose will say something about the product and the company that makes it. Apple has always had a light, near-irreverent personality in its Macintosh ads, while IBM has tended toward a more staid, professional feel. Geico Insurance began life with a straightforward, hard-hitting approach, later trading it in on a humorous, off-the-wall feel. Robitussin takes a warm, comforting personality, while NyQuil takes a more whimsical approach.

A few cautions are in order.

When you're agreeing on the tone your advertising will take, I suggest the word *professional* be disallowed. I cringe when clients tell me to position them as "the professionals," for two reasons. One reason is that the word is meaningless. When was the last time you heard someone say, "Wow! These guys are *professionals!* They're the ones for me!" With everyone generously applying the word to themselves in their advertising, including grease-covered teenagers in the lube pit and plunger-wielding people who unclog your toilet, it has been robbed of all meaning. Consumers pay it no heed, and rightly so. The other reason is that people who are obsessed with conveying a professional image tend to mistake an absence of personality for professionalism. Thus, they end up refusing to allow headlines and copy with punch. They don't—excuse me, *do not*—allow contractions or even conversational language in their copy. They tend to be satisfied only when they have pruned every trace of humanity from their image. What they miss is that no one—not even other professionals—likes doing business with cadavers.

Many companies want to be funny. Humor is difficult to pull off. What's more, that which is funny to you may come across as silly, offensive, or simply incomprehensible to others. Think of people you know who only *think* they're funny. There is nothing more pathetic.

It's safer to use whimsy than to attempt humor. People react well to a company that doesn't mistake itself for a comedy show yet doesn't take itself too seriously, either. For a community bank client offering online banking services, we used the headline, "Bank in your pajamas." Not a knee-slapper, but not alienatingly dead-serious, either.

Should your brand take on the personality of a spokesperson, you run the risk of the spokesperson's dying, and the brand personality with it, as was the case when Wendy's Dave Thomas passed away. You also run risks if the spokesperson gets into trouble. Pepsi couldn't drop Michael Jackson fast enough when child molestation charges arose.

Tone should be relevant. Toughness is not something consumers want in a fabric softener or a sleep aid, but it is something they want very much in a stain remover or a snow tire.

Remember that the purpose of tone is to *connect*, not to show off. This is not a time to think about how you want to look. Nor is it a time to impress your honors English teacher with literary devices like alliteration or with esoteric words like *esoteric* (and, for that matter, *alliteration*). It's a time to focus on what will reach your market.

STICK WITH IT

Once you've built your strategy, stick with it for the long haul.

That doesn't mean you need to stick with the same execution with every ad. Headlines, layouts, and copy approaches can change. But it does mean your market, means of motivating them, objectives, key claim, proof of key claim, other claims, and tone should remain consistent.

It's not as easy as it may sound. Chances are you'll find yourself tiring of your strategy long before you launch it, much less once you're months or even years into it. It's important to remember that your market doesn't live with your advertising day in and day out the way you do. You can only hope they'll be exposed to it enough to tire of it.

I am not, however, telling you not to measure, adjust, fine-tune, and improve. You should do all of those things on an ongoing basis. But to abandon a strategy that's working simply because you're tired of it is foolhardy.

SUMMARY POINTS FROM
THE DISCIPLINE OF STRATEGY

- A solid strategy isn't necessary for really cool advertising, but it's essential for *successful* advertising.

- Shortchanging the strategic process is one of the top reasons advertising fails.

- A good strategy begins with defining and understanding your target.

- Set objectives. You can evaluate effectiveness only if you define what you hope to accomplish. The more specific your objectives are, the better.

- "To get our name out there" isn't an objective at all.

- Identify one key point above all others. Then challenge it. What makes you think it will move people to action?

- An unsubstantiated claim is an empty boast. Decide how your messaging will back up the key claim.

- List other claims your strategy will include.

- You can find hidden benefits by using the words *so you*.

- Define the tone your messages will take.

- Do not define your tone with meaningless words like *professional*.

- Once you have a winning strategy, stick with it.

12

S cience can dissect just about anything.

That song you love? Science can map out rhythms, frequencies, and overtones and show you the physics behind every note. The painting you love? Science can analyze how the light reflected from its surface travels through your eye's rods and cones to your brain, which interprets the resultant electrical impulses as an image. That speech that moved you? Science can explain how words create imagery, which stimulates the brain to release endorphins into your system.

One might think that, with enough analysis and replication, science might at some future date render flesh-and-blood artists obsolete.

But I don't think so.

OF SCIENCE AND ART

Science can indeed analyze and, to an extent, explain art. But it has limits when it comes to the *execution* of art. For that, you still need an artist.

Take dancing. You can scientifically catalog steps and moves, matching them to their corresponding beats. *But science can't make dancers.* If you took 1,000 random people and taught them every step and move until each person developed proficiency, only a certain number would end up actually *dancing*. The rest would be regurgitating moves. The average observer would be able to tell the dancers from the move-regurgitators just by watching.

You can provide 1,000 people the same cooking skills and recipes, but only some will turn out perfect soufflés. You can teach 1,000 people when to press the piano keys, but only some will make music. You can teach 1,000 people drafting and building design, but only some will produce architecture that takes your breath away.

So it takes more than isolating what goes into art to produce what *is* art. While this may change at some future date, right now all the science in the world cannot duplicate a basic ingredient of human accomplishment. And, ironically, this ingredient makes science itself possible.

It's called *talent*.

INNATE ABILITY

Talent is innate ability.

We normally associate talent with the visual and performing arts, but talent is manifest in other arenas. Talent is what lets some people make intuitive sense of Einstein's Theory of Relativity (both Special and General), while most shake their heads in confusion. It lets some people list the ingredients of an entrée upon one taste, while the best most people can do is ask, "What kind of sauce is that?" It lets some people make speeches that move crowds to action, while most people avoid public speaking altogether. It lets some people send a football spiraling flawlessly across the field after minimal instruction, while others struggle to toss the darn thing 10 feet.

Clearly, to perform some tasks better than average, talent is a requirement.[1]

I submit that *marketing* is an art that, to perform it well, requires innate ability.

Talent.

A TALENT FOR ASKING "WHAT IF . . . ?"

Imagination is a talent that is vital in science—and in marketing.

Science can test a hypothesis, but to have a hypothesis to test, someone must first dream enough to ask, "What if . . . ?"

Electrical current didn't inevitably lead to light bulbs, *Penicillin notatum* didn't inevitably lead to antibiotics, and carnival pitchmen didn't inevitably lead to direct response television advertising. In each case, it took a Thomas Edison, an Alexander Fleming, or an Alvin Eicoff to observe, wonder, and test.

Likewise, imagination in marketing is important. It's what leads the designer to say, "What will happen to sales if I make the package easier to open?" It's what makes the distributor say, "Maybe we'll sell more if we put the product at eye level." It's what makes the marketer sit bolt upright in the middle of the night and exclaim (perhaps scaring the daylights out of a spouse), "Maybe we should position this as a product for young women starting their careers instead of for men about to retire!"

I believe that the art of imagination is a talent. A gift. You and I have both known too many visionless but otherwise brilliant people, and too many artistic but otherwise clueless people, to believe otherwise.

To make progress in marketing or in any other science, we must have more than a lab. We must have smart but talented people who challenge the status quo.

A TALENT FOR TESTING

Developing a talent for seeing possibilities and saying, "What if . . . ?" is the vital first step. But to blindly chase hunches without subjecting them to the rigors of valid scientific testing can lead to costly mistakes. Even for the talented.

Valid scientific testing itself requires talent. Because humans are given to jumping to conclusions ("That painting I did on the cave wall caused the buffalo to walk within range of my spear"), it takes talent to step back and challenge assumptions.

Devising valid tests also requires talent. It's far too easy and tempting to unwittingly set up a test with a built-in, self-fulfilling prophecy. Like the executive who says, "I'll show the ad to my [like-minded] friends and see what they think of it."

I hope you remember from Chapters 8 and 9 that conducting focus groups and telephone interviews to ask people what they think of your idea doesn't qualify as "the rigors of valid scientific testing." What does? Let's look at a condensed version of the scientific method.

Science starts with a filtered hunch. "Filtered" because there simply isn't time or need to test every hunch.

Common sense is a readily available filter. If your vice president of product development suggests a new line of intimate apparel with the name "Itches Like Hell," you needn't do much research to dismiss it.

Still, caution when filtering is advised. Common sense often misleads. Common sense initially reeled at the idea of steamboats, the Alaska Purchase, Federal Express, Vivien Leigh as Scarlett O'Hara, and Daniel Craig as James Bond. Your common sense may initially reel at the idea of making what appears already clear on a Web page, like a button marked "Contact us," even more clear, by changing it to read "Click here to contact us." Yet the longer version usually pulls more clicks. You may like how the click-here button looks in blue, especially if blue is one of your brand colors, but changing it to red is likely to increase clicks.[2]

Doing homework serves as a more reliable filter. Study valid tests conducted by other marketers, particularly *direct response* marketers. These are the folks who test and measure sales results of every web site, e-mail, print advertisement, broadcast spot, and direct mailing. If direct marketing pros consistently report—and they do—that magazine ads on the right-hand page with a coupon in the lower right-hand corner perform better than magazine ads on the left or with coupons in any other position, then you can count on it. These folks know.

If you read Chapter 7, you understand the importance of reading marketing books with a "suitably jaundiced eye." Be particularly wary of authors who build their cases anecdotally. Anecdotal evidence raises questions but proves nothing. Look instead for tests that can be replicated and validated.

A hunch that survives filtering intact is what scientists call a *hypothesis*.[3] If after suitable filtering you believe you're on to a winning hypothesis, it's time to . . .

Set up an experiment. Or, more simply, a test to see if your hypothesis holds up. For a valid test, you'll need to observe some rules.

Rule One: Keep your test groups no larger than what's required for a valid sample. The idea is to rule out non-performing ideas, approaches, and techniques without investing a fortune each time. When you happen upon a winner, retest to rule out happenstance. If it still performs, back *that* with increasingly bigger budgets.

Rule Two: Decide *in advance* on outcomes that will confirm or disprove your hypothesis. A good question to ask yourself is, "What would I expect to see happen if my hypothesis is correct?" This is important, because hindsight bias beguiles and blinds. If your hunch is that paying for the rights to use a popular song in your commercial will increase sales by more than the cost of the song rights, you must be prepared to admit failure if sales do not increase by more than that amount—no matter how much the revised spot increases product awareness, and no matter how many awards it wins for best score.

Rule Three: Isolate what you wish to test. If a purple background with sans serif type outsells a green background with serif type, you won't know whether the background or the font made the difference. That means you'll need a way to track sales directly back to each version of each ad or campaign. There are ideas for this in Chapter 9.

Rule Four: Have a *control group*. If a sales increase (or decrease) follows the implementation of your idea, a control group provides the only means of determining whether your idea was truly responsible for the change.

Your control group should be representative of your market, and it must not be exposed to your campaign. Then, if a test group exposed to the campaign buys more per capita, you'll know your campaign deserves the credit. If the control and test groups buy at the same rate, the campaign had no effect. If the control group buys at the higher rate, your test campaign may be driving sales *down*.[4]

At the very least, you'll need this information to keep the bean counters at bay. When you achieve a sales upsurge, the bean counters are likely to assert that it would have happened anyway, campaign or no campaign, and suggest diverting your marketing budget to other purposes. Control groups are your only defense.

Rule Five: Your test must be something that you and others can replicate. That way, you can rule out happenstance and remain open should things change.[5]

Trust the results. Even if they contradict what you'd hoped to prove, and even if they strike you as counterintuitive. Maybe the flashy web site doesn't produce as many unique visitors as the plainer one that loads faster. Maybe the folksy, entertaining copy doesn't win as many sales as the straight-talk one. Maybe the sleek black packaging you prefer doesn't sell as well as the white glossy packaging you find boring. But fair is fair. Advocates of the straightforward must be prepared to acknowledge when the flashier approach outsells the mundane one.

Trusting results is easier said than done. For one client, we tested three offers to motivate purchase: a flashlight, airline miles, and an entertainment center remote control. Want to guess which was the winner before reading on? I bet on the remote. My client bet on the air miles. When results were in, the flashlight was the clear winner. My client and I were both wrong. Because we were so convinced of how we expected things to turn out, it was not easy for us to accept the numbers. But we retested and the results held, so we sighed, gave up our pet offers, and rolled out the flashlight offer.[6]

There may be times when, after repeated failures, you'll find it's time to give up. I recently met with a client and agreed with him that it was time to do just that. We had tried numerous markets, offers, and appeals—and no one was buying. Whether the product simply wasn't viable or ours was the wrong agency to promote it, it was time to quit throwing good money after bad. Not a pleasant fact for either of us to face, but a necessary one. The good news was that our modest testing allowed us to reach the conclusion *without* spending big dollars.

But on the positive and more frequent side, I've also seen modest testing against a control allow marketers to significantly increase sales, without increasing the marketing budget, by being able to isolate what works—and then do more of it.

A TALENT FOR EXECUTION

Suppose you have the talent to wonder, "What if our ad campaign appealed to people's desire for short-term gain instead of their need for long-term security?" And suppose you have the talent to set up a valid test to learn which approach sells more.

Good so far, but *crafting the appeal itself also requires talent*. You may know what the campaign should convey, but someone must now craft the copy to hold and persuade. Someone must design the look to attract eyes to the right elements in the right order.

This is what we call *creative talent*. And just as all the scientific analysis in the world cannot make dancers out of people with no sense of rhythm, analysis of copy and layout won't rescue the creatively inept.

Famous, sales-producing ads that survived testing and proved themselves in the market were first the products of talented artists with vision. John Caples, who was without question an advertising scientist, *could* have written an ad for a mail-order piano course that read, "Learn to play the piano in your spare time." Instead, a talented Caples came up with the record sales-producing and, today, legendary headline: "They laughed when I sat down at the piano—but when I began to play!" David Ogilvy, a research aficionado previously employed by Gallup, *could* have written, "This Rolls Royce features an incredibly quiet ride." But instead, talent kicked in and he dramatized the point this way: "At 60 miles per hour, the loudest sound you can hear in the new Rolls Royce is the ticking of the electric clock." Aflac *could* have run an ad campaign saying, "When your employer offers us as supplementary insurance, remember you've heard of us." Instead, a talented creative team came up with the lovable duck unforgettably screaming, *"Aflac!"* at us from our TV sets.[7]

Science can test ideas like these. But only artists can cook them up.

FUZZY LINE

Some might argue that there is a fuzzy line between the art of marketing as I've described it here and what some people might call the very gut intuition I've argued against throughout this book.

But I don't think so. The art of marketing explores, while gut intuition retreats to the safe and familiar. The What-If

Talent wonders what might happen if you change your look, the Testing Talent devises a way to find out, and the Artistic Talent creates and presents—while the gut says, "Better not, this is scary," or "I like it, so let's go with it."

The marketing artist is disciplined and open to discovery. Gut intuition is self-indulgent and dogmatic.

So encourage the art of marketing. Nurture and reward it as you subject it to scientific scrutiny.

But beware that fuzzy line. Wanton creativity is *fun*. It's alluring. I've seen it drag intelligent people from a rational approach and straight to an irrational one in a heartbeat.

A good first step toward arming yourself against the wanton creativity allure is to implement the scientific method as presented here. Once you've done that, *build a solid marketing strategy* around it. One that keeps you on course.

Don't let the word *disciplined* with reference to good marketing artistry put you off. If you're a good creative talent, you'll come up with great work. A disciplined strategy won't—can't—stop you. Instead, it will *ensure that your great creative work is on target and accomplishes its objective.*

Not only will you produce work that's admired, you'll produce work that inspires people to take action. Few artists can make *that* claim.

SUMMARY POINTS FROM
THE ART OF SCIENTIFIC MARKETING

- There is a science to marketing, but there is an art to good science.
- When you're willing to subject your talent to the rigors of the scientific method, you get the best of both worlds.

- A good hypothesis is a filtered hunch.
- A representative sample is necessary for reliable conclusions.
- Before the experiment, determine the results that would validate or invalidate your hypothesis.
- Isolate what you're testing.
- Control groups eliminate happenstance as an explanation of results.
- Nonfalsifiable assertions are not science but dogma. A test should be repeatable, remaining open to challenge and new information.
- Trust results. Even counterintuitive ones. Even if they offend your artistic sense.
- The marketing artist is disciplined. Gut intuition tends to be self-indulgent.

Endnote

Remember when I asked you to check your gut intuition at the marketing department door? I hope you have done so, and that in its place you will henceforth commit your marketing to good judgment, science, and talent within a framework of critical thinking, testing, disciplined strategy, and value-driven branding practice.

Leave your gut intuition unemployed. Never again hand it the car keys while you nap in the back seat.

After a while, your gut will quit whining. This is a good thing. Who knows? You might just invent marketing history's next breakthrough campaign.

Notes

Preface

1. Of course, we have it both ways. We tell companies to increase marketing when sales are up, too.
2. Hence the phrase "exception that proves the rule." It doesn't mean that an exception is a de facto *validation* of a rule; it means that an exception places a rule under scrutiny.

Chapter 1   What Any Fool Knows

1. There is some dispute as to who conducted the original experiment. Tradition favors Galileo.
2. For a thorough and entertaining look at astrology from a scientific point of view, see Richard Wiseman, Ph.D., *Quirkology: How We Discover the Big Truths in Small Things* (New York: Basic Books, 2007), and Philip Plait, Ph.D., *Bad Astronomy: Misconceptions and Misuses Revealed, from Astrology to the Moon Landing "Hoax"* (Hoboken, N.J.: John Wiley & Sons, 2002).
3. There's nothing new about ascribing healing powers to magnets. Dr. Franz Anton Mesmer (1735–1815) attempted to treat ailments by hanging magnets on his patients. His legacy is our modern word *mesmerize*, and extant quacks in our day who make money selling so-called therapeutic

magnets to unwary hopefuls. Sometimes, but not often enough, they are reined in. In early 2008, the FTC cracked down on the Illinois-based marketer of the "Q-Ray Ionized Bracelet" to the tune of up to $87,000,000 in court-ordered refunds. Visit *randi.org/joom/content/view/145/27/ #i17* and see "Justice Is Served."

4. If cold weather caused colds, we'd have a hard time explaining the occasional cold caught in summer. Notwithstanding the fact that we do catch more colds in winter, cold weather doesn't cause them. It motivates us to spend more time indoors, which creates more opportunities to catch and transmit viruses.

5. The chocolate-acne connection is no more than an enduring myth. If you don't believe me, Google "causes of acne" and read up for yourself.

6. If you refuse to concede that your hat doesn't have magical properties that help your game, fine. But surely you can see that *other* people's claims to a lucky hat are bogus, can't you?

7. In advertising circles, this is a brilliant though probably, in defense of its proponents, an unwitting circular argument: that strong sales in the wake of a creative campaign are proof of the power of creativity, that poor sales indicate the campaign wasn't truly creative after all, and that both further prove that only truly creative advertising sells.

8. Note the emphasis on *consistency*. We must allow for and rule out flukes. We're not interested here in what works once, but in what works reliably. The success of one Pet Rock does not make a science any more than one person's recovery from cancer after swallowing linseed oil capsules constitutes a cure.

9. Their findings are by no means a closely guarded secret. They are readily available to anyone who wishes to research them. (See Recommended Readings at the end of this book.) Yet for reasons beyond me, the advertising community at large ignores the information.

10. Not that the trend runs unopposed. At the same time our nation develops a passion for debunking pseudoscience, an equal and opposite reaction seems to arise in the form of clinging to superstition and ignorance to govern public policy. But such discussion inevitably leads to politics. I'll stick with marketing for now.

11. Cited in the highly recommended book by Michael Shermer, *The Mind of the Market: Compassionate Apes, Competitive Humans, and Other Tales from Evolutionary Economics* (New York: Times Books, 2007).

Chapter 2   *Your Gut Doesn't Know Squat*

1. Yes, there's something to the claim about nose-touching and lying. See David J. Lieberman, Ph.D., *Never Be Lied to Again*, (New York: St. Martin's Press, 1998).

2. Ford proved them wrong by building a hugely successful company. But his opponents proved themselves right by building a successful company of their own, later named General Motors. So two sets of guts disagreed, and both ended up being right. And wrong.

3. So-called fortune-tellers do much the same thing. Those who honestly believe they have powers mistake for clairvoyance a gift for picking up and correlating subtle physical clues—a facial expression, eyes looking one way when improvising and another when recalling, a locket, fidgeting, sitting up or slouching in response to warm and cold answers, and so on. There are also out-and-out frauds who knowingly read clues, not to

mention avail themselves of accomplices, clandestine research, and carnival tricks.

4. Though I pretended to no gift, like any good magician, I didn't reveal the secret. Instead, I asked for her phone number, which, to my amazement, she gave me. Here the story ends. A mind-reading trick in the shoe department was one thing. Having to make real, post-show conversation was altogether another. As I said, I wasn't an adept flirt. I chickened out and never called her.

Chapter 3   Leaps

1. In 2000, Universal Pictures immortalized Brockovich and the PG&E case in a movie bearing her name and starring Julia Roberts.

2. Michael Fumento, an attorney specializing in science and health, has written extensively on the subject. Visit his web site: fumento.com. For information specific to Brockovich (including responses from her), see fumento.com/erinwsj.html. Also see Leon Jaroff, *Erin Brockovich's Junk Science*, at time.com/time/columnist/jaroff/article/0,9565, 464386,00.html.

3. Let's be generous and concede that marketers as a group tend to be intelligent people, individual exceptions notwithstanding.

4. Just in case I convinced you, I should point out right now that the earth both spins and orbits the sun.

5. I suppose I should have counted my blessings, since normally in such circumstances the excuse is, "The ad agency did a poor job."

6. In the book by Robert Wright, *The Moral Animal: Why We Are the Way We Are* (Gloucester, MA.: Peter Smith, 1997), the author says that blaming aggression on testosterone

is like blaming fires on fire trucks. Both arrive after the fact.

7. We resigned the account in less time than we spent pursuing it.

8. Filmmaker Jean Cocteau said, "We must believe in luck. For how else can we explain the success of people we don't like?"

9. He also fell victim to a misconception about how sex does and doesn't sell. See Chapter 10, "The Sciences Cast a Light on Marketing."

10. Lest you accuse me of proffering anecdotal evidence in defense of premium offers, I should add that these results are not atypical. Test after test reveals that solid offers consistently increase response. This outcome is not limited to tests performed at RESPONSE. That is why the offer of a premium is standard direct marketing practice.

11. I'm not going to get into theology here. Debunking marketing mythology is sacrilegious and risky enough.

12. For a more complete discussion of this particular god of the gaps, see Chapter 5, "The Great Creativity Debate."

13. It worked.

14. For more on research errors and how to avoid them, see Chapters 8 and 9.

15. Focus groups are absolutely *not* the way to solve this kind of dilemma. Never ask people to predict what they would do. They haven't a clue. (You really must read Chapters 8 and 9 on research.)

16. Who was right? We'll never know. There was no additional testing.

17. Autism *diagnoses* have indeed increased over the past few decades, but that doesn't mean autism itself has increased. For one thing, professionals are more alert to the

condition than in earlier years and thus recognize and diagnose it with greater frequency. For another, the definition of autism has broadened. Once-excluded conditions
like high-functioning autism and Asperger's syndrome
are now counted in the statistics. Finally, well after the
accused ingredients were removed from vaccines, diagnoses of autism continued unabated. All of this logic
does nothing to assuage the hearts of parents who naturally want to know *why* their kids are autistic. The best
answer we have right now is, "We don't know."

Chapter 4 Beguiled by Correlation

1. The Coca-Cola Company, President Bill Clinton, Tom
   Cruise, and Martha Stewart, respectively.
2. This myth may come from the 1958 Disney film *White
   Wilderness*, in which a few hapless lemmings were
   crowded over a ledge by their fellows. The filmmakers
   represented it as mass, self-induced drowning and as a
   regular event.
3. With a look through police records, John Stossel debunks this one in his enjoyable and highly readable
   book *Myths, Lies, and Downright Stupidity: Get Out the
   Shovel—Why Everything You Know Is Wrong* (New York:
   Hyperion, 2006).
4. According to a study appearing in the *New England
   Journal of Medicine* in 1979, statistics land squarely on
   the side of random distribution when it comes to births
   and lunar phases. In the book by Thomas Gilovich, *How
   We Know What Isn't So: The Fallibility of Human Reason in
   Everyday Life* (New York: Free Press, 1993), the author
   reveals the cognitive errors to which humans are prone
   en route to arriving at, and fiercely defending, misconceptions like this one.

5. According to Morton Hunt, *The Story of Psychology* (New York: Anchor Books, 1994), Vicary's admission to the fraud appears in a 1984 article in *Advertising Age*.

6. Next time you read an article that tells you people don't read long advertisements, I'd like you to consider something: How long was the article you read telling you no one reads long stuff?

7. Not to imply that lengthy copy ensures readership. Important, interesting, readable copy helps.

8. It's easy to suppose that direct marketers purchase late-night time because it costs less than prime time. That's actually just a happy coincidence. Marketers who move their 800-number spots to prime time end up spending more and selling less.

9. I visited with a friend who was working on an ad for a bank. The bank was offering a free TV to everyone who opened a home equity line of credit. My friend had some very clever, attention-getting lines. Still, I couldn't resist suggesting he add a conspicuous "Free TV with a home equity line of credit." His answer was very interesting: "That's the trouble with you direct marketing guys. You just *say* it."

10. More on testing in Chapter 9.

11. It's possible that painting a buffalo psyches you for the hunt, subconsciously leading you to make a better effort, in turn leading to better results. The error occurs in attributing a better hunt to *magic*.

12. Otherwise, because *most* teens consume violent media, *most* teens would become violent. But *most* do not. Saying violent entertainment makes teens act out is like saying that thinking about sex causes cancer in adults because most adults with cancer have thought about sex.

13. Coal is porous, so it transfers heat to other objects, like feet, slowly. If the bed of coals isn't too long and you don't dally, you can fire-walk any time you wish, without positive-thinking coaches like Tony Robbins. Just be sure to use the same kind of coals he uses. Do not under any circumstances try walking across a bed of heated pieces of steel. You would suffer serious damage with your first step.

14. I pick on Harry Beckwith, *Selling the Invisible* (Dublin, Ireland: Business Plus, 1997) and other popular books from time to time. (Just wait till you get to Chapter 7.) I still recommend them as enjoyable, thought-provoking reads. Just don't mistake Beckwith's or other authors' anecdotes and conclusions for gospel. Or worse, for science.

15. This and other documented studies of shopping behavior are found in Paco Underhill's engrossing and useful book, *Why We Buy: The Science of Shopping* (New York: Simon & Schuster, 1999).

16. The dry cleaning chain has fewer than 20 stores. But when it comes to database marketing, this company exhibits more acumen than some of our largest clients.

17. This and the two preceding points are cited in Underhill, *Why We Buy.*

18. January is the month in which people *make* resolutions. The fact that most lose no time in *breaking* them helps successive Januarys remain equally profitable for diet plans and other resolution-related products.

19. We know this from ongoing optimization tests by firms like Optimost, LLC, in San Jose, California.

20. The most comprehensive list I've found so far is Nat G. Bodian's book, *Direct Marketing Rules of Thumb: 1,000 Practical and Profitable Ideas to Help You Improve Response, Save Money, and Increase Efficiency in Your Direct Program*

(New York: McGraw-Hill, 1995). For other titles, see the Recommended Readings in the back of this book.

Chapter 5   *The Great Creativity Debate*

1. In the book by John Caples, *Tested Advertising Methods* (Paramus, N.J.: Prentice-Hall, 1998), he talks about testing the headlines "How to Repair Cars" and "How to Fix Cars." When results rolled in, it was clear that 20 percent more people preferred to *fix* their cars.

2. For what it's worth, the French word *avertissement* means *warning*.

3. The competitor was stuck with a genuine white elephant that had cost him a fortune and now had no value. Yes, that's the origin of the expression.

4. These tales of Barnum are found in the book by James B. Twitchell, *Twenty Ads That Shook the World: The Century's Most Groundbreaking Advertising and How It Changed Us All* (New York: Three Rivers, 2000), an enjoyable and informative synoptic history of advertising. For a more comprehensive history of advertising, I recommend Stephen Fox, *The Mirror Makers: A History of American Advertising and Its Creators* (New York: Morrow, 1984).

5. The advertising and mail-order industries aren't the only ones to clean up their acts over time. Quite a few of today's respected drug companies, medical practices, oil conglomerates, food purveyors, philanthropic organizations, and other businesses had shady origins themselves. Sadly, scamming the public isn't limited to our past. Even today, flimflam companies make a fortune peddling medically worthless products—homeopathic "medicines," natural "cures," "therapeutic" magnets, and so on. Their marketing

would make patent medicine vendors of yore proud. They get away with it because their products fall outside FDA regulation, and because, after making what surely *resembles* a host of medical claims, they include tiny type in ads and on labels that says, "No specific medical claim is made." One can only hope that the gaps in our legal system that allow such folks to continue in business will close soon.

6. For marvelous tales of early direct response TV advertising, chase down a copy of the out-of-print book by Alvin Eicoff, *Or Your Money Back* (New York: Crown, 1982).

7. The ad dramatized the stringent standards a VW Beetle had to meet before shipment: The copy revealed that an inspector wouldn't pass the car because of a blemish on a chrome strip adorning the glove compartment.

8. I can already hear the ad agencies object, "Creativity may be commonplace, but *true* creativity, like the kind *we* do, isn't." My response: Give me a break.

9. Before going on, let me add that I hope you read Chapters 3 ("Leaps") and 4 ("Beguiled by Correlation"). They provide helpful background.

10. "Near certainty" is about the best science can do. That's why theories are called *theories* and not *facts*. By definition, a theory is falsifiable, meaning you can test it and verify it—or debunk it—for yourself. It's a great system that helps keep science honest by allowing it to revise its positions as new knowledge emerges. Politicians and other dogmatists could learn a thing or two from this.

11. See Chapter 9, "How to Predict a Marketing Success."

12. Good direct response marketers perform valid testing as a matter of course, which makes direct response the closest thing we have to real marketing science.

13. With a sufficiently broad definition, you'll be able to link creativity with more than just sales. You'll be able to link it with cancer cures, favorable weather, horoscopes, and UFO sightings. This is due to the Law of Truly Large Numbers, which I discuss in Chapter 7.

14. I regret that such a study is not possible. There are too many campaigns and too many factors to allow isolation and representative samples—especially after the fact. It's better to build controls and measures in *before* launching a campaign.

15. I have owned three German Shepherds. All utter wimps.

16. For a more complete discussion of what a brand is and isn't, see Chapter 6, "A Critical Look at Branding."

17. Or were those ideas creative, after all? Though obvious to me, those were breakthrough ideas to my clients. That's the trouble with a subjective standard like "creativity." It's hard to pin down. Yet if you define it after the fact—for example, what succeeds was creative, what didn't wasn't—you end up with a *tautology* (a fancy word for a circular argument).

18. I'm skeptical about Danny's claim, but not about the point he was trying to make. In fact, there *is* a bit of art and science to auto mechanics, and to marketing. See Chapter 12.

19. You don't hear this Bernbach quote quite as often.

20. It's arguably unfair to call these ads uncreative. Joe Sugarman and other direct response megastars will tell you their work is *extremely* creative. They have made an art and science of presenting products in a way that makes people reach for their wallets and their phones. "Uncreative" in this sense simply means "not the kind of creativity the advertising industry honors with the likes of Clio Awards."

21. You would be right to observe that I just served up a list of anecdotes, right after telling you that anecdotes aren't proof. So let me add that these cases, though not proof in and of themselves, are illustrative of the proof that is found in statistically valid data from over a century of direct marketing testing.

Chapter 6   A Critical Look at Branding

1. I would like to suggest a slogan for slogans using the word *people:* The *Default* Slogan. Or, The *Who Do You Think You're Impressing?* Slogan. Sticking *people* in your slogan will not humanize you or endear you to the reader. Nor will it make you unique, unless your competitors begin using slogans like, "Proudly hiring the worst," "We only hire feral cats," or "To hell with people." When was the last time you rewarded a merchant with your business because of a gratuitous line about people making the difference, putting people first, people serving people, or people working to make people happier in people places made by people for people?

2. Time for a diatribe on the subject of slogans. I'll begin by admitting that there *is* such a thing as a good one. (Who can argue with "When it absolutely, positively, has to be there overnight"?) But bad ones abound, thanks to people who think an ad is only complete with a would-be zinger and a TM (apparently to ensure no one steals "Where quality counts").

   Bad slogans are not exclusive to amateurs, as a look through a national magazine attests. It seems that Cottonelle Ultra bathroom tissue is "Looking out for the family." I had no idea toilet paper could do that, but I feel safer already. Competitor Scott Extra Soft is "Common sense on a roll." I hope they avoid that line on radio, where *sense* might sound like the more truthful but not very pleasing *scents*. United Healthcare's tagline is, "It only makes sense." What's good for toilet paper is good for health insurance.

The U.S. military tagged its ads with the unwieldy but inarguable, "The qualities you acquire in the military are qualities that stay with you for life." This tagline even had its own tagline: "See it for what it really is." It sounds defensive, even for a Department of Defense, but at least our military's ads come with "Two taglines for the price of one"—an example of "Your taxes at work."

Then there's the *just-in-case-you-missed-it-we'll-say-it-again* slogan. Dannon Light 'n Fit tags their ads, "Eat Light 'n Fit. Be Light 'n Fit." If only they could have worked the product name into the tagline one more time.

Chips Ahoy's cookies pack "A whole lotta yum," which sure beats a half lotta yum. Dole offers this uplifting thought about canned peaches: "Life is sweet." Speaking of life, Life cereal's ad ends with, "Life is full of surprises." I dug through the box in our cupboard, but found only cereal. Maybe that was the surprise.

3. The unnamed magazine referred to in Note 2 carries an abundance of both awareness and direct response ads. Nearly every awareness ad in the issue I examined sported a tagline. None of the direct response ads did. Given that the response ads are measured down to cost-per-response and awareness ads usually aren't, it may be telling that direct-response writers generally don't bother writing taglines at all.

4. Not that image-only branding has lost all of its power. Some people still agree to pay for the privilege of wearing a Rolex watch, even though it keeps time no better and may have fewer features than a $50 rival, or for a

Rolls Royce that reaches its destination no faster than a used, rusted Dodge.

5. Not that the erosion of brand image is solely responsible for Marlboro's decline. Government restrictions on cigarette advertising played a significant part.

6. I'm not suggesting that your company *doesn't* care. It's just that "We care" should be demonstrated, not claimed. When was the last time you heard Nordstrom brag about great customer service? A strong brand *shows*, by its behavior, more than it *tells*.

7. "Masked Logo," "Fickle Customer," Oh, Come On," "Value Statement Transplant," and "Do Your Employees Get It?" are trademarks of the RESPONSE Agency, Inc., for its brand evaluation tests.

8. No one is immune from self-delusion, and that includes Yours Truly. When my firm had only five employees, I was convinced that we were all on the same page when it came to values. With so few of us in such close, daily contact, how could it have been otherwise? But one day when I bragged to a consultant, "Everyone here knows what we stand for," my associates looked dumbfounded and said, "No, we don't." If that was possible with a staff of five, imagine what kind of disconnect is possible in larger organizations.

Chapter 7 *Beware the Experts*

1. Cited in Robert Todd Carroll, *The Skeptic's Dictionary* (Hoboken, N.J.: John Wiley & Sons, 2003), a highly readable, encyclopedic volume. And thanks go to Mike Zukerman of Insurance.com, who politely took me aside and corrected me during a break at one of my seminars. I'd been misquoting Carroll and using the wrong number. It really is 23.

2. Lest you find that unlikely, look at it this way. Suppose you gather 365 people at random. To *avoid* any two of them sharing a birthday, every person you selected would have to have been born on a different day of the year from the other 364. The odds of that happening are far lower than of ending up with a few matches.

3. For more information about successful people who mistake their good fortune for expertise, please read Nassim Nicholas Taleb's delightful book, *Fooled by Randomness: The Hidden Role of Chance in Life and in the Markets* (New York: Texere, 2004).

4. Assuming, that is, one can correctly identify just what those steps were in order to include only the important ones and exclude the unimportant ones. To do so requires clairvoyance beyond the abilities of most marketing consultants and authors, despite what they may think of themselves.

5. See Chapters 8 and 9 for tips on testing and strategy.

6. I discuss selection bias in Chapter 3, but it deserves special mention in the context of business how-to books.

7. Arden presents cases in which people found success doing the opposite of what anyone else would do, thereby contending that contrariness is the overriding principle. (Such advice can be hard to follow if half the people you know do one thing and the other half do the other.) Readers may recall an episode of *Seinfeld* in which character George Costanza found uncanny success adopting a similar approach. Somehow, we find the idea laughable in a sitcom, but we are expected to take it seriously in a business book.

8. Missing the point, a number of companies began talking up excellence in their advertising. This was to the bewilderment of consumers who hadn't read the book,

whose own definition of excellence may have differed from that of the marketers, and who didn't really care if a company rated itself as excellent or not.

9. A recurring problem with subjective "data" of these sorts is that it can be and usually is used to defend opposing positions.

10. At the time Thomas J. Peters and Robert H. Waterman wrote *In Search of Excellence* (New York: Harper and Row, 1982), Microsoft failed to qualify as an "excellent" company. It wasn't yet ten years old.

11. Both books do allude to "comparison companies." Unfortunately, these companies were selected and evaluated by the same arbitrary process as the "excellent" and "great" companies.

12. The "excellent" business practices the authors cite were interview-generated, thus anecdotal, and therefore prove nothing. (See Chapter 3, "Leaps.") To make matters worse, in the introduction to *In Search of Excellence*, the authors disclaim contradictory anecdotes readers may have of their own about the practices of "excellent" companies. In other words, anecdotes supporting the authors' conclusions are valid. Anecdotes to the contrary are not.

Chapter 8   *Help Stop Research Abuse*

1. In case you missed it, Truman won.

2. A paragraph should be not one word longer or shorter than what it needs to be to convey its meaning.

3. Beckwith credits the case study to authors Horace Schwerin and Henry Newell, who write about it in their book, *Persuasion in Marketing: Dynamics of Marketing's Great Untapped Resource* (New York: John Wiley & Sons, 1981).

4. An actual market test might have shown the features-oriented spot to be the more effective version after all. Direct response marketers have long known that when it comes to selling big-ticket items, the more relevant information you provide, the more you sell. They know this not because they asked people to predict their behavior but because they tested long and short ads in the actual marketplace. As a general rule, long ads perform better. This is why successful mail-order ads for high-end products are always longer than typical awareness ads, and successful direct response TV spots are always 60, not 30 seconds.

5. Casino operators have another trick to keep people playing slot machines, which I share at the risk of admitting that human beings have something in common with rats. Rats fast lose interest in a lever that always delivers food. But when a lever delivers only small bits of food and only at random, the rats can't seem to leave it alone. Likewise, slots that deliver random, tiny "wins" keep people feeding machines their coins and pulling levers.

6. Bear with me. That "other means" is the subject of the next chapter.

7. You may be surprised to learn that it is the *left* brain that tells stories, since tradition has it that the *right* brain is more creative, and that lefthanded people (who are supposedly more right-brained) tend to be more creative than righthanded people. New evidence from brain scans suggests otherwise. Many brain functions, including creativity, do not occur in one exclusive spot, but fire up multiple brain centers in concert. Notwithstanding, the left brain on its own appears to have the corner on rationalizing.

8. Pinker's book, *The Blank Slate: The Modern Denial of Human Nature* (New York: Penguin, 2003), deals with genetics, neuroscience, and environment in the nature-nurture debate. The applicability of his material to marketing, corporate policy, hiring, and managing, however, makes it one of the best business books I've ever read.

9. For more neurological surprises, read the book by V. S. Ramachandran and Sandra Blakeslee, *Phantoms in the Brain: Probing the Mysteries of the Human Mind* (New York: HarperCollins, 1998).

10. See Lenore Skenazy: "But Wait, There's More: How Infomercial Guru Gets His Ideas," *Advertising Age*, February 25, 2008.

11. Some defenders of the craft will assure you that a good moderator can control the influence of dominant personalities in a focus group. I have two objections to that assertion. One, it's oxymoronic. If a moderator is controlling the dynamics of the group, you're not getting honest feedback from the group. Two, no matter what a moderator may claim, there's only so much anyone at any skill level can do to tame a lion and bolster a mouse in the same room within a one- or two-hour span.

12. The experience of a personal acquaintance illustrates the power of peer pressure in focus groups. She participated in a focus group that was shown a drawing. After the drawing was removed, the moderator asked how many participants had seen a tiger in the drawing. She hadn't seen it, but other group members insisted it was there. It wasn't long before she recalled seeing the tiger after all. She later learned that this wasn't a real focus group. It was an experiment designed to test the power of peer pressure to induce a false memory. It turned out that she was the test subject. And there was no tiger.

Chapter 9   How to Predict a Marketing Success

1. From Perry W. Buffington, Ph.D., *Cheap Psychological Tricks: What to Do When Hard Work, Honesty, and Perseverance Fail* (Atlanta: Peachtree Publishers, 1996).

2. Use of the Heisenberg Uncertainty Principle here is symbolic, not literal. A particle changes its behavior when it's bombarded with photons because the impact of the bombardment makes it do so—not because it knows you're watching.

3. This joke normally singles out one of many religious organizations that prohibit alcohol consumption. Rather than choose which religion to offend, I made the joke generic.

4. Even with conclusive tests like this one, irrationality can slip in. At first, the client was reluctant to retire the less effective spots. They asked, "What if we miss a chance to sell to someone who would only have responded to one of the less effective spots?" We explained that the point was to capitalize on the commercial that sold the most at the lowest cost per sale, not to provide equal opportunity to viewers of varying taste.

5. Tests often reaffirm my own gut's fallibility. The version I was certain would win was, in fact, the one that lost. Unfortunately, it was also the version I wrote. My associate Ty Kiisel wrote the winner. To make matters worse, he was gracious about having outdone me.

6. A recent accident drove home to us the power of targeting. A client that sells annual memberships assigned us to send a notice telling lapsed members their privileges had expired—but accidentally furnished us a mailing list of members in good standing. Although this was the *wrong* list, the mailing produced record results—28 times the response from the *right* list. Of

course, there could be no follow-up test to see whether threatening expiration of privileges to members in good standing was a viable strategy. Lying to customers is never permissible, nor is it wise. Even if it might be profitable.

7. For other great books on tested advertising, see "Recommended Readings" at the end of this book.

8. And sometimes that's exactly what happened. Alas.

9. If you'd rather not risk conducting this experiment on your own, you can read about it in Jay Ingram, *The Science of Everyday Life* (New York: Viking, 1990).

Chapter 10   The Sciences Cast a Light on Marketing

1. The term for a heritable behavioral trait is *instinct*. Most people have no trouble with the concept of instinct in animals. Scientists who go a step further and claim human behavior is evolved and heritable have sparked angry reactions. The fear is that such information could be used to excuse criminal behavior or racial discrimination. Nonsense. The importance of holding people accountable and the *rightness* of treating them morally, ethically, and fairly do not hinge on whether behavior is learned or evolved.

2. Behaviors like washing before meals or after shaking hands with someone who has a cold, reading books, and obeying traffic laws do not come naturally to us. We learn them.

3. The fashions we wear, the jargon we use, and the music we like are examples of learned behaviors that are dynamic and strongly influenced by society.

4. Like sprouting goose bumps when cold or frightened, seeking shelter from the elements, eating when we're hungry, or protecting our children.

5. DNA evidence reveals that today's house dogs—all breeds—were domesticated from Asian wolves some 17,000 years ago.

6. I had that problem with a German Shepherd named Hudson. I knew he wasn't coming up short in the housebreaking department; he was just going overboard in the deference department. Knowing that eye contact and my height could intimidate, I dropped to all fours and backed toward him. (Fortunately, no neighbors were watching.) It worked. Hudson greeted me dry and reassured. I was eventually able to resume walking into the room like a normal human, with no recidivism on Hudson's part.

7. It could be argued that in the socioeconomic environment we have fashioned for ourselves, those who prove fittest at such tasks indeed rise to the top.

8. For insights into how moving away from the tropics may have led some groups to invent farming, create advanced weapons, and form large cities while those remaining behind didn't, see Jared Diamond, *Guns, Germs, and Steel: The Fates of Human Societies* (New York: W. W. Norton, 2005).

9. By contrast, fast-reproducing organisms like viruses and bacteria evolve faster than we can keep up with them with vaccines and other measures.

10. I must spoil the fun of anyone who hopes to excuse bad behavior with "My genes made me do it." Genes may nudge us in a direction, but we still have minds that can veto the nudge.

11. For a brilliant book on fossil DNA, see Sean B. Carroll, *The Making of the Fittest: DNA and the Ultimate Forensic Record of Evolution* (New York: W. W. Norton, 2006).

12. Not that any of this is conscious. If sexual selection drives our purchase habits, we are no more aware of it

than of the fact that natural selection makes us care for our eyes by blinking 6.25 million times per year.

13. It sounds so much more . . . well, *psychological.*

14. There is strong evidence that signaling preceded speech in humans. To take one example, "Broca's area" in the human brain controls the muscles used for speech as well as those used for hand gestures; damage to Broca's area can disable both. This and like tidbits are found in the insightful and highly readable book by Matt Ridley, *The Agile Gene: How Nature Turns on Nurture* (formerly *Nature via Nurture,* New York: HarperCollins, 2003).

15. Even the average, honest citizen is likely to push the speed limit or zip through the occasional yellow light— unless a police car is in sight.

16. Like Betty Crocker, Mrs. Olsen, and even the Keebler Elves.

17. It has been and, in some circles, still is fashionable to blame our vices upon society. The fact is that society, far from being the villainous creator of our unsavory inclinations, deserves credit for giving us less destructive alternatives. Competition, lawsuits, negotiations, business, embargos, and spectator sports are more mannerly, better organized forms of warfare. But the substitution is neither complete nor universal. All people, cultures, and nations have work to do. Some more than others.

18. A marketer can only hope to attain such fierce loyalty, but as yet no one seems to have cracked that particular code by design, only by serendipity. Brands like the Saturn automobile or the Song airline that have attempted to create an out-of-the-box following have failed and embarrassed themselves in the process.

19. Note to anyone who believes in the power of subliminal messaging: Don't. It's a fraud. It has failed every
scientific test. Cases you've heard about that were "proven" are either bogus or urban legends.

Chapter 11   The Discipline of Strategy

1. California advertising icon Jerry Della Famina was
known for characterizing advertising as "the most fun
you can have with your clothes on."
2. Among others, see *vmrintl.com/Ref_art/women_buy.htm*
and *blogs.consumerreports.org/cars/2007/03/women_car_
buyer.html*.
3. Sometimes building positive awareness can be a viable
goal. If you're an oil excavator and you don't want to be
accused of raping the environment, an awareness campaign showing the pains you take to keep the landscape
pristine is a good idea. But too often, *awareness*, quanti-
fied or not, is a wimpy, worthless, cop-out objective.
With sufficient budget or attention-getting antics,
awareness is easy to attain. Getting people to take action that you can measure at the cash register is harder
to do, and often a worthier use for your marketing
budget.
4. From John Lyons, *Guts: Advertising from the Inside Out*
(New York: Amacom, 1987).
5. Pepsi's taste tests, arguably convincing and successful
in boosting grocery store sales, had only the appearance of good research. For more information, read
Malcolm Gladwell, *Blink: The Power of Thinking Without
Thinking* (New York: Little, Brown, 2005).
6. Which, incidentally, isn't an example of feature-versus-
benefit at all. "Quarter-inch hole" is no more than a re-
statement of "quarter-inch drill bit." A better example

would be, "People don't buy hats; they buy looking swanky, or they buy protection from the sun."

Chapter 12   *The Art of Scientific Marketing*

1. Many companies remove the need for talent at the production level. It might take talent to invent a tasty Egg McMuffin, but once it's invented, you can create a McMuffin-making system that just about anyone can run.

2. What works on the Web still changes fast enough that I tend to qualify every observation about it with "as of this writing."

3. In everyday language, people tend to use *hypothesis* and *theory* interchangeably. Let's not. A hypothesis is your best guess *after* weighing information but *before* doing an experiment. If you can draw predictive, reliable conclusions after the experiment, you may be on your way to a theory.

4. It happens. If P. T. Barnum really said all publicity is good publicity, he was mistaken. Sales went down during Alka Seltzer's fondly remembered "I can't believe I ate the whole thing" campaign. More recently, sales declined throughout Taco Bell's popular Chihuahua campaign and during Miller Brewing Company's well-liked "Man Law" campaign. And even though Nissan experienced a dismal launch of their Infiniti line with commercials showing scenery instead of the car, Hyundai tried a similar strategy in 2007—and sales dropped.

5. Some things indeed change. For decades, Courier font was a requirement in direct mail sales letters; thanks to the computer, other fonts are now acceptable for all but the most senior readers. Some things change *very* fast: The days with the highest click-through rates for blast

e-mails, for instance, change as fast as marketers discover and gang up on them. But some things have never changed and may never. Good copy alone still outsells great graphics alone—in any medium.

6. I'm wrong about what will work best more often than I care to admit. More evidence that gut intuition just can't be given free rein—even my own well-experienced gut intuition.

7. More recently, Aflac announced plans to scale back the awareness objective and its campaign, duck and all, for direct selling objectives.

Recommended Readings

Here is a list of books from which I drew a good deal of inspiration as *Prove It Before You Promote It: How to Take the Guesswork Out of Marketing* began to take shape.

You'll find only a handful of them in the business section of your bookstore. For the others, you'll have to comb the science section.

Please take the trouble. Some of the best books I've read about management and marketing weren't meant to be management and marketing books and they weren't written by business people. They are books about human cognition, neurology, and evolution, and they are written by scientists. Mercifully, the particular scientists whose work I stumbled upon also happen to be highly skilled, readable writers. If you're good at reading for implication as well as information, you'll find it well worth your while to visit the science section more often.

Bodian, Nat G. *Direct Marketing Rules of Thumb: 1,000 Practical and Profitable Ideas to Help You Improve Response, Save Money, and Increase Efficiency in Your Direct Program.* New York: McGraw-Hill, 1995.

Buffington, Perry W. *Cheap Psychological Tricks: How to Get What You Want and Be Happy.* New York: MJF Books, 1996.

Caples, John. *Tested Advertising Methods.* Paramus, N.J.: Prentice-Hall, 1998.

————. *How to Make Your Advertising Make Money.* Englewood Cliffs, N.J.: Prentice-Hall, 1983.

Carroll, Robert Todd. *The Skeptic's Dictionary: A Collection of Strange Beliefs, Amusing Deceptions, and Dangerous Delusions.* Hoboken, N.J.: Wiley, 2003.

Carroll, Sean B. *The Making of the Fittest: DNA and the Ultimate Forensic Record of Evolution.* New York: W. W. Norton, 2006.

Chialdini, Robert. *Influence: The Psychology of Persuasion.* New York: William Morrow, 1993.

Eicoff, Alvin. *Or Your Money Back.* New York: Crown, 1982.

Diamond, Jared. *Guns, Germs, and Steel: The Fates of Human Societies.* New York: W. W. Norton & Company, 1999.

Fox, Stephen. *The Mirror Makers: A History of American Advertising and Its Creators.* New York: William Morrow, 1997.

Grant, John. *Discarded Science: Ideas That Seemed Good at the Time.* Church Farm House, Surrey, UK: Facts, Figures & Fun, 2006.

Gilovich, Thomas. *How We Know What Isn't So: The Fallibility of Human Reason in Everyday Life.* New York: Free Press, 1991.

Huff, Darrell. *How to Lie with Statistics.* New York: W. W. Norton, 1982.

Hunt, Morton. *The Story of Psychology.* New York: First Anchor, 1993.

Ingram, Jay. *The Science of Everyday Life* (revised edition). Toronto: Penguin Canada, 2006.

Levitt, Steven D. and Dubner, Stephen. *Freakonomics: A Rogue Economist Explores the Hidden Side of Everything.* New York: HarperCollins, 2005.

Lieberman, David J. *Never Be Lied to Again.* New York: St. Martin's Press, 1998.

Ogilvy, David. *Ogilvy on Advertising.* New York: Crown, 1983.

Pinker, Steven. *The Blank Slate: The Modern Denial of Human Nature.* New York: Penguin, 2003.

_____. *How the Mind Works.* New York: W. W. Norton, 1997.

Plait, Philip. *Bad Astronomy: Misconceptions and Misuses Revealed, from Astrology to the Moon Landing "Hoax".* New York: Wiley, 2002.

Rackham, Neil. *Spin Selling.* New York: McGraw-Hill, 1995.

Ramachandran, V. S. and Blakeslee, Sandra. *Phantoms in the Brain: Probing the Mysteries of the Human Mind.* New York: HarperCollins, 1998.

Ridley, Matt. *The Agile Gene: How Nature Turns on Nurture.* New York: HarperCollins, 2003.

Sagan, Carl. *The Demon-Haunted World: Science as a Candle in the Dark.* New York: Ballantine, 1996.

Shermer, Michael. *The Mind of the Market: Compassionate Apes, Competitive Humans, and Other Tales from Evolutionary Economics.* New York: Times Books, 2007.

_____. *Science Friction: Where the Known Meets the Unknown.* New York: Henry Holt, 2005.

_____. *The Science of Good and Evil: Why People Cheat, Gossip, Care, Share, and Follow the Golden Rule.* New York: Henry Holt, 2004.

_____. *Why Darwin Matters: The Case Against Intelligent Design.* New York: Henry Holt, 2006.

_____. *Why People Believe Weird Things: Pseudoscience, Superstition, and Other Confusions of Our Time*. New York: Henry Holt, 1997.

Sowell, Thomas. *The Vision of the Anointed: Self-Congratulation as a Basis for Social Policy*. New York: Basic Books, 1995.

Stossel, John. *Myths, Lies, and Downright Stupidity: Get Out the Shovel—Why Everything You Know Is Wrong*. New York: Hyperion, 2006.

Taleb, Nassim Nicholas. *Fooled by Randomness: The Hidden Role of Chance in Life and in the Markets*. New York: Texere, 2004.

Twitchell, James B. *Twenty Ads That Shook the World: The Century's Most Groundbreaking Advertising and How It Changed Us All*. New York: Three Rivers, 2000.

Underhill, Paco. *Why We Buy: The Science of Shopping*. New York: Simon & Schuster, 1999.

Wiseman, Richard. *Quirkology: How We Discover the Big Truths in Small Things*. New York: Basic Books, 2007.

Wright, Robert. *The Moral Animal: Why We Are the Way We Are: The New Science of Evolutionary Psychology*. New York: Vintage Books, 1994.

Zaltman, Gerald. *How Customers Think: Essential Insights into the Mind of the Market*. Boston: Harvard Business School Press, 2003.

Index